M000026850

The Four-Blocks®
Literacy Model

The Administrator's Guide to the Four Blocks®

by
Dorothy P. Hall
and
Patricia M. Cunningham

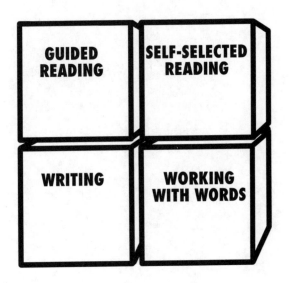

GUIDED READING

SELF-SELECTED READING

WRITING

WORKING WITH WORDS

Carson-Dellosa Publishing Company, Inc.
Greensboro, North Carolina

Credits

Editor:
Joey Bland

Layout Design:
Joey Bland

Cover Design:
Matthew VanZomeren

ISBN 0-88724-978-7

Preface

It was the 1989-1990 school year when Four Blocks was first piloted in one first-grade classroom at Clemmons Elementary in North Carolina. Ten years later, we did a Four-Blocks census and found that teachers were using this framework in hundreds of classrooms and schools across the country and in other countries as well. Since we began, we have met many wonderful teachers who have discovered the Four-Blocks framework in a number of different ways and then made changes in their instruction to match the model. How did these teachers find out about the Four Blocks? We found that teachers either read the first article we wrote in the *Reading Teacher* titled, "Non-Ability Grouped, Multimethod Instruction: A Year in a First-Grade Classroom." (44, pp. 566-571), heard us speak at a seminar or workshop, chatted on the Four-Blocks mailring on the World Wide Web, or read *Classrooms That Work* (Cunningham and Allington, 1994, 1999). The teachers then began to put the framework into practice in their classrooms. For some teachers, this happened long before we wrote our first books about Four Blocks in the mid-1990s.

As we continued to work with teachers, schools, and school systems who were using the Four-Blocks framework in classrooms across the country, we recognized that administrators and teachers needed checklists reflecting what we have learned about the model over the past thirteen years. We are indebted to many Four-Blocks friends, also presenters, who read our drafts, commented, and helped to make sure we covered all the Four-Blocks practices teachers wanted to know about and many of the adaptations teachers make to suit the children they teach. Some of these presenters are still teachers who talk about Four Blocks when they can; others have left the classroom to talk about Four Blocks full time. Among those who helped are Amanda Arens, Karen Loman (who wrote *The Administrator's Guide to Building Blocks™* with Dottie Hall), Deb Smith, Tom Roe, and DeLinda Youngblood. There have been others who helped make this book a reality because of the questions they asked and the conversations they had with us over the years. We are indebted to all of them for their help.

Table of Contents

Table of Contents

The Administrator's Guide to the Four Blocks®
Introduction

How and Why the Four-Blocks® Literacy Model Was Developed

The Four-Blocks framework was developed by teachers who believed that to be successful in teaching ALL children to read and write, we were going to have to do it ALL! "Doing it all" means incorporating on a daily basis the different approaches to reading. The Four Blocks—Guided Reading, Self-Selected Reading, Writing, and Working with Words—represent four different approaches to teaching children to read. Daily instruction in all four blocks provides numerous and varied opportunities for all children to learn to read and write. Doing all four blocks acknowledges that children do not all learn in the same way and provides substantial instruction to support whatever learning personality a child comes with. The other big difference between children—their different literacy levels—is acknowledged by using a variety of during-reading formats and before- and after-reading activities to make each block as multilevel as possible, providing additional support for children who struggle and additional challenges for children who catch on quickly.

The Four-Blocks framework began in 1989-1990 in one first-grade classroom (Cunningham, Hall, and Defee, 1991; Cunningham, Hall, and Defee, 1998). In the 1990-1991 school year, 16 first-grade teachers in four schools used the framework, making modifications to suit a variety of different school populations, including a Title 1 school (Hall, Prevatte, and Cunningham, 1995). Since 1991, the framework has been used in numerous first-, second- and third-grade classrooms where many children still struggle with reading and writing. For more information about the Four-Blocks® Literacy Model, see: *The Teacher's Guide to the Four Blocks®* by Cunningham, Hall, and Sigmon (Carson-Dellosa, 1999, 2001); *Month-by-Month Phonics for First Grade*, *Month-by-Month Phonics for Second Grade*, or *Month-by-Month Phonics for Third Grade* by Cunningham and Hall (Carson-Dellosa, 1997 and 1998); *Guided Reading the Four-Blocks® Way* by Cunningham, Hall, and Cunningham (Carson-Dellosa, 2000); and *Self-Selected Reading the Four-Blocks® Way* by Cunningham, Hall, and Gambrell (Carson-Dellosa, 2002).

The Four-Blocks framework has many variations, but there are two basic principles that must be followed if reading and writing instruction can truly be called Four Blocks. First, because we believe the idea that children learn to read in different ways, each block gets 30-40 minutes of instruction each and every day. Providing enough time and equal time to each block assures that children are given the same opportunity to become literate regardless of which approach is most compatible with their individual learning personalities. The second basic principle is that, while we don't put children in fixed ability groups, we make our instruction as multilevel as possible so that average, struggling, and excelling students all learn to read and write at the highest possible level. Doing the four blocks every day and giving them approximately equal time is a simple matter of making a schedule and sticking to it. Making the instruction in each block as multilevel as possible is more complex, but it can be done and you will see many examples throughout this book.

Because 30-40 minutes each day for each block is a basic principle, we do not see Four Blocks as the appropriate organizational framework for kindergarten or for most intermediate grades. We do believe that children in every grade level should receive instruction in guided reading, self-selected reading, writing, and words, but for kindergarten and intermediate grades, the schedule would look quite different.

Building Blocks—A Framework for Kindergarten

We call our kindergarten program Building Blocks, and we integrate guided reading, self-selected reading, writing, and words with the themes and units that are part of every kindergarten day. The blocks don't have a set time slot—and certainly don't each get 30-40 minutes every day. Four Blocks is a primary-grades framework that is consistent with how primary teachers teach and schedule their day. Building Blocks is a kindergarten framework that is consistent with how kindergarten teachers teach and structure their day. The blocks we want to "build" in kindergarten are: the Desire to Read and Write, Language Concepts, Print Concepts, Phonemic Awareness, Interesting Words, and Letters and Sounds. We build these blocks by:

- Reading to children (both fiction and nonfiction).
- Reading with children (predictable big books and interactive charts).
- Providing opportunities for children to read by themselves.
- Writing for children (morning messages at the start of the day).
- Writing with children (predictable charts and interactive morning messages).
- Providing opportunities for children to write by themselves.
- Developing phonemic awareness (the oral).
- Working with letters and sounds, or phonics (the written).
- Helping kindergarten children learn some interesting-to-them words (names, environmental print, etc.).

These activities are the basis of the kindergarten model. For more about Building Blocks, see: *Month-by-Month Reading and Writing for Kindergarten* by Hall and Cunningham (Carson-Dellosa,1997); *The Teacher's Guide to Building Blocks™* by Hall and Williams (Carson-Dellosa, 2000); and *The Administrator's Guide to Building Blocks™* by Hall, Arens, and Loman (Carson-Dellosa, 2002).

Big Blocks—A Framework for Upper Grades

Time allocation is also where we change the Four-Blocks framework for upper grades. Because we view each block as an approach to reading and because we have seen children in every Four-Blocks classroom for whom each block is their best road to literacy, we take our beginning readers down all four roads every day. However, by the time children have achieved a fluent third-grade reading and writing level, they read and write well enough that we change the time allocations. Once children can read and write fluently at third-grade level, they have well-developed phonics and spelling skills, so that Working with Words no longer gets one-quarter of their literacy instructional time. Working with Words instruction in the intermediate grades focuses on big words, most of which come from science, health, and social studies. Self-Selected Reading still gets a scheduled 30-40 minutes each day, but Guided Reading and Writing get longer blocks. Much of Guided Reading and the focused-writing component of the Writing Block are integrated with the content subjects of science, health, and social studies. Because our intermediate framework focuses on big ideas and big words from subject areas and includes big blocks of time for content integration, we call our intermediate framework "Big Blocks." For more information on Big Blocks, see: *Month-by-Month Phonics for the Upper Grades* by Cunningham and Hall (Carson-Dellosa, 1998), *Guided Reading the Four-Blocks® Way* by Cunningham, Hall, and Cunningham (Carson-Dellosa, 2000), and *Self-Selected Reading the Four-Blocks® Way* by Cunningham, Hall, and Gambrell (Carson-Dellosa, 2001).

In some upper-grades classrooms, many children do not read and write fluently at the third-grade level. Perhaps they have not gotten appropriate instruction, have moved from school to school, or are just learning English. For these classrooms, the Four Blocks, with roughly equal instructional time allocated to each of the approaches, would still be the most appropriate and effective organizational framework. The issue is not the grade level of the students—but the students' reading levels. Until children read and write fluently at third-grade level, we believe they need a minimum of two hours of literacy instruction each day and equal attention to each of the four major approaches.

The Four Blocks

Self-Selected Reading

Historically called "individualized reading" or "personalized reading" (Veatch, 1959), many teachers now label their self-selected reading time "Reader's Workshop" (Routman, 1995). Regardless of what it is called, self-selected reading is that part of a balanced literacy program when children get to choose what they want to read and what parts of their reading they want to respond to. Opportunities are provided for children to share and respond to what is read. Teachers hold conferences with children about the books the children are reading.

The goals of the Self-Selected Reading block are:

- To introduce children to all types of literature through the teacher read-aloud.
- To encourage children's reading interests.
- To provide instructional-level reading.
- To build intrinsic motivation for reading.

In Four-Blocks classrooms, the Self-Selected Reading block includes a teacher read-aloud during which the teacher reads to the children from a wide range of literature. Next, children read on their own levels, choosing from a variety of materials, including the widest possible range of topics, genres, and levels. While the children read, the teacher conferences with one-fifth of the class each day. The block usually ends with a few children sharing their books with the class in a "reader's chair" format, but this is not mandatory.

Self-Selected Reading is, by definition, multilevel. The component of self-selected reading that makes it multilevel is the fact that children choose what they want to read. In Four-Blocks classrooms, teachers read aloud different types and levels of materials on different topics and then make the whole range of reading materials available to students. During the weekly conferences, teachers support children's choices and help children choose books for next week that they can read and will enjoy. For more information on Self-Selected Reading, see: *Self-Selected Reading the Four-Blocks® Way* by Cunningham, Hall, and Gambrell (Carson-Dellosa, 2002).

Guided Reading

Guided Reading lessons usually have a before-reading phase, a during-reading phase, and an after-reading phase. Depending on the text being read, the comprehension strategies being taught, and the reading levels of the children, Four-Blocks teachers use a great variety of before-, during-, and after-reading variations. Before children read, teachers help them build and access prior knowledge, make connections to personal experiences, and develop vocabulary essential for comprehension. Four-Blocks teachers also teach comprehension strategies, including connecting, predicting, summarizing, monitoring, inferring, and evaluating. After reading, teachers help children connect new knowledge to what they knew before, discuss what they learned, follow up the comprehension strategy taught, and discuss how they are becoming better readers by using their reading strategies.

In Four-Blocks classrooms, children read the selections in different formats. On some days, the whole class reads together and the teacher uses shared reading, choral reading, echo reading, or ERT . . . (Everyone Read To . . .) to encourage all students' active participation. On other days, the children may read the selection in partners, Playschool Groups, Book Club Groups, or Literature Circles. Sometimes, teachers may pull out small coaching groups and read a selection with them while the other children read the selection in partners or individually. Four-Blocks teachers vary the format depending upon the material to be read and the amount of support children need to read the material.

The goals of the Guided Reading Block are:

- To teach comprehension skills and strategies.
- To develop background knowledge, meaning vocabulary, and oral language.
- To teach children how to read all types of literature.
- To provide as much instructional-level reading as possible.
- To maintain the motivation and self-confidence of our struggling readers.

Guided Reading is the hardest block to make multilevel. Any selection is going to be too hard for some children and too easy for others. Because all states give all children the same reading test with grade-level passages, we think that all children should be exposed to some grade-level material. The comprehension strategies taught during Guided Reading are practiced in both below grade-level and grade-level materials. Children also use these strategies when reading on their own levels during the Self-Selected Reading block. Teachers have shared with us many clever ways they have devised for making Guided Reading more multilevel. Here are some of the more common multilevel strategies:

- Guided Reading time is not spent only in grade-level material. Rather, teachers alternate selections—one at the average reading level of the class and one at an easier reading level.
- In Book Club groups, teachers select four books tied together in some way. In selecting these books, they include one that is a little easier than average and one a little harder than average.
- Teachers and students reread each selection—or parts of longer selections—several times, each time for a different purpose in a different format. Rereading enables children who couldn't read it fluently the first time to achieve fluent reading by the last reading.
- Children who need help are not left to read by themselves but are supported in a variety of ways. On some days, children read with partners or in Playschool Groups. On other days, teachers meet with small coaching groups, and children learn how to coach each other to figure out words and meanings.
- On some days, some children read the selection by themselves and others read with partners while the teacher meets with a small group. These small coaching groups change regularly and do not include only the low readers.
- Some teachers schedule their Guided Reading time when they have "help" coming. Guided Reading can be more multilevel if you have more adults working with coaching groups or circulating and providing support to partners or groups.
- Teachers also provide some extra easy reading time for children whose reading levels are well below even the easier selections read during Guided Reading. Some teachers meet with children individually or in small groups while the rest of the children are engaged in centers or other activities. Some teachers also include good reading models in a "Fun Reading Club" or "After Lunch Bunch." The most struggling readers are included more often.
- When available, teachers coordinate with early intervention teachers and/or tutors to provide Guided Reading instruction on appropriate levels.
- Some teachers spread out their struggling readers across the days for Self-Selected Reading conferences. They conference first with these students each day, giving them a little extra time and making sure they select books they will enjoy and can read.

One way or another, Four-Blocks teachers make sure that children are getting the support they need, including some coaching each week, as they read material at their instructional level. For more information on Guided Reading, see: *Guided Reading the Four-Blocks® Way* by Cunningham, Hall, and Cunningham (Carson-Dellosa, 2000).

Writing

The Writing Block includes both self-selected writing in which children choose their topics, and focused writing in which children learn how to write particular forms and on particular topics. Children are taught to use process writing to improve their first drafts so they don't have to think of everything at one time. Process writing is carried out in "Writer's Workshop" fashion (Graves, 1995; Routman, 1995; Calkins, 1994). The Writing Block begins with a 10-minute mini-lesson, during which the teacher writes and models all the things writers do when writing. Next, the children go to their own writing. They are at different stages of the writing process—finishing a story, starting a new story, editing, illustrating, etc. While the children write, the teacher conferences with individuals who are getting ready to publish. Each day, this block ends with "author's chair," during which several students share works in progress or their published works.

The goals of the Writing Block are:

- To view writing as a way of telling about things.
- To write fluently.
- To apply grammar and mechanics in their own writing.
- To learn particular writing forms.
- To learn to read through writing.
- To maintain the motivation and self-confidence of struggling writers.

Writing is the most multilevel block because it is not limited by the availability or acceptability of appropriate books. Because Four-Blocks teachers allow children to choose their own topics, accept whatever level of first-draft writing each child can accomplish, and allow them to work on their pieces as many days as needed, all children can succeed in writing. As teachers help children publish the pieces they have chosen, they have the opportunity to truly "individualize" their teaching. Looking at the writing of a child usually reveals both what the child needs to move forward and what the child is ready to understand. The writing conference provides the "teachable moment" in which both advanced and struggling writers can be nudged forward in their literacy development. For more information on Writing the Four-Blocks way, see: *The Teacher's Guide to the Four Blocks®* by Cunningham, Hall, and Sigmon (Carson-Dellosa, 1999, 2001); *Writing Mini-Lessons for First Grade* by Hall, Cunningham, and Boger (Carson-Dellosa, 2002); *Writing Mini-Lessons for Second Grade* by Hall, Cunningham, and Smith (Carson-Dellosa, 2002); and *Writing Mini-Lessons for Third Grade* by Sigmon and Ford (Carson-Dellosa, 2002).

Working with Words

In the Working with Words Block, children learn to read and spell high-frequency words and learn the patterns that allow them to decode and spell a lot of words. The first 10 minutes of this block are usually used for reviewing the word wall words. Students practice new and old words daily by looking at them, saying them, chanting the letters, writing the words, and self-correcting the words with the teacher.

The remaining 15-25 minutes of Working with Words time is used for an activity which helps children learn to decode and spell. A variety of different activities are used on different days. Some of the most popular activities are Rounding Up the Rhymes, Making Words, Reading/Writing Rhymes, Using Words You Know, Word Sorting and Hunting, and Guess the Covered Word. For grade-level-specific descriptions of Working with Words activities, see: *Month-by-Month Phonics for First Grade* by Cunningham and Hall (Carson-Dellosa, 1997); *Month-by-Month Phonics for Second Grade* by Hall and Cunningham (Carson-Dellosa, 1998); and *Month-by-Month Phonics for Third Grade* by Cunningham and Hall (Carson-Dellosa, 1998).

The Administrator's Guide to the Four Blocks® © Carson-Dellosa CD-2425

The goals of the Working with Words Block are:

- To learn to read and spell the high-frequency words.
- To learn how to decode and spell many other words using patterns from known words.
- To automatically and fluently use phonics and spelling patterns while reading and writing.

Activities in the Working with Words Block are multilevel in a variety of ways. During the daily word wall practice, the children who have learned to read the words being practiced are learning to spell them. Other children who require lots of practice with words are learning to read them.

Making Words, Rounding Up the Rhymes, Reading/Writing Rhymes, Using Words You Know, and other Working with Words activities are also multilevel. Most lessons begin with short, easy words and progress to longer, more complex words. Children who still need to develop phonemic awareness can do this as they stretch out words and decide which words rhyme. Each lesson includes some sorting of words into patterns, then using those patterns to read and spell some new words. Children with different levels of word knowledge see how they can use the patterns they see in words to read and spell other words. These children also learn that rhyming words usually—but not always—have the same spelling pattern. All lessons provide review for beginning letter sounds for those who still need it.

Connecting the Blocks to Each Other and the Rest of the Curriculum

Each of the Four Blocks has its scheduled time in every classroom. But, Four-Blocks teachers also make many links among the four blocks and to other areas of the curriculum. Some of the links most commonly made include:

- In first grade, selecting high-frequency words, which were included many times in one of the Guided Reading selections, to the word wall.
- Doing a Guess the Covered Word activity using a paragraph that will soon be read as part of the Guided Reading selection.
- Rounding Up the Rhymes from a book or poem read during Guided Reading or Self-Selected Reading.
- Teaching a Making Words lesson using an important word from Guided Reading as the secret word.
- During the first part of Self-Selected Reading, reading aloud to children a selection which "sets them up" for an author, genre, or topic they will soon be reading during Guided Reading.
- Making books read during Guided Reading Book Club groups available for children to choose during Self-Selected Reading.
- Choosing a topic for the writing mini-lesson which relates to something read during Guided Reading.
- Doing some focused-writing lessons in which children learn to write in a genre they have read during Guided Reading.
- Choosing materials for Guided Reading that fit the current theme or a science, health, or social studies topic.
- Reminding children to try strategies taught during Guided Reading as they read their Self-Selected Reading books.

What Does a Four-Blocks Classroom Look Like?

In a Four-Blocks classroom, you are likely to see:

- Desks or tables arranged so that four, five, or six children sit together and can work with partners or as a group when needed.

- A carpeted area or rug where students gather together close to the teacher for teacher read-alouds, writing mini-lessons, and small groups.

- Books placed in baskets, wash tubs, or arranged on shelves for students to read at Self-Selected Reading time.

- Other reading materials such as magazines, newspapers, big books, child-authored books, etc., placed where children can easily find and read them.

- An overhead projector or chart paper for the daily writing mini-lesson and other activities.

- Students' work displayed on bulletin boards in the room and outside the room; student and class-made books arranged on shelves, in baskets or tubs, and on tables.

The Administrator's Guide to the Four Blocks®   © Carson-Dellosa CD-2425

- A word wall under the letters of the alphabet, with words written on colored paper and printed large enough for children to read the words no matter where they are sitting in the room.
- A pocket chart for Making Words and other Working with Words and Guided Reading activities.
- Theme boards or charts with vocabulary words for themes, seasons, or topics the class is studying or talking and writing about (but words that students won't use all year, therefore they shouldn't be put on the word wall).
- An editor's checklist which is added to as the year goes on.
- Writing materials for writing and publishing, including different kinds and shapes of paper; crayons, pens, pencils, markers, and computers for composing and illustrating stories, informational pieces, and published books; and stapler or bookbinder for book making.
- Some teachers find a timer useful for keeping the blocks an appropriate length and to keep the pace brisk during some lessons.
- Teachers working with children in a variety of whole-class, small-group, and one-to-one conferences.
- Students actively engaged and hopefully having fun!

Why an Administrator's Guide to the Four Blocks?

This book is meant to serve as a valuable resource for both administrators and first-, second-, and third-grade teachers who want to organize their instruction in the Four-Blocks® Literacy Model. We hope that administrators will find it a valuable tool to understand the Four Blocks and help teachers succeed with the model. Our goal is to help administrators learn the model and know what to look for when they observe teachers doing any of the Four Blocks. Administrators can also use these checklists as the basis of the follow-up discussions with teachers after watching a Four-Blocks lesson and conferencing with the teacher they observed.

How Can Teachers Use These Checklists?

This book is also a resource for teachers who, after reading one or all of the Four-Blocks® Literacy Model books, still want to know if they are doing the activities right, what they could improve, and what they might not be doing but would like to include.

Planning for Staff Development

There are a number of ways teachers become familiar with the Four-Blocks framework. The most popular way is attending a Four-Blocks workshop or seminar in your area or a Four-Blocks/Building-Blocks Conference in North Carolina. Some schools or school systems hire a Four-Blocks presenter to provide a workshop for all their teachers. In doing so, the school or system is sure that every teacher gets the same experience, but some "trainers" or presenters are better than others. While some claim to be "trainers" because they have attended one or two Four-Blocks training sessions, they have not had enough experience with the model to help others. Others claim to be trained in Four Blocks, but do not present the model correctly to teachers and administrators, and thus confuse rather than help teachers. So buyers beware! There are no "train the trainer" models for Four Blocks, Building Blocks, and Big Blocks. There are many wonderful teachers, former teachers, and former administrators who offer this training, though. A list of presenters can be found on the Four-Blocks Web site at *www.wfu.edu/~cunningh/fourblocks*.

When helping teachers learn to do Four Blocks, it is best to have separate sessions in Building Blocks for kindergarten teachers, in Four Blocks for teachers in grades 1-3, and in Big Blocks for upper-grades teachers. Other ways teachers learn about Four Blocks are by reading the Four-Blocks books and other professional books about reading and writing. Teachers learn best when they have opportunities to discuss these ideas and activities with one another, with experienced Four-Blocks teachers, or with the many teachers on the Four-Blocks mailring at *www.teachers.net*.

How much training a teacher needs depends upon the teacher, his or her knowledge of early reading and writing practices, and his or her past experiences. Extensive training is not necessary for many teachers who have kept up with the latest research and methods. Many teachers learn as they teach, and the basic books (*The Teacher's Guide to the Four Blocks®* and the appropriate grade-level book from the *Month-by-Month Phonics* series) can provide ongoing support. When a teacher wants more knowledge on a topic, staff development can and should be provided. Often schools or school systems have teachers who can provide this help locally. If not, a presenter usually can be found and hired by a school, two or more schools training together, or a school system. Introducing teachers to the model is just the beginning. Some teachers need ongoing support. Administrators can take advantage of weekly grade-level meetings before, during, or after school to provide staff development for teachers who want help or feel there is an activity or Block they want to know more about.

Once you decide that Four Blocks is what you want to do in your classroom or school, then some staff development is usually necessary. Often teachers in a school or school system who know what good instruction is, have asked for some Four-Blocks training. These same teachers are just the teachers who can help you decide what your needs at a school are.

Training sessions that have worked wonderfully in some schools are:

- A one-day workshop or seminar on the Four Blocks (presenter should cover all four blocks that day).
- A two-day, in-depth workshop on the Four Blocks (more than two days at one time usually puts teachers on "overload" unless one day is devoted to lesson planning and "make and take").
- A workshop on each of the Four Blocks (spaced a week or two apart).

Supporting the Four Blocks

Many times, schools build their staff development for the year on more than one new idea, program, or set of standards that must be addressed. Teachers can become overwhelmed if they are asked to do too much at one time—especially primary teachers who are responsible for teaching all of the subjects to all of their children. For successful implementation of the Four-Blocks framework, teachers need to be focused on the Four-Blocks framework. Other areas of the curriculum are not likely to be slighted; usually good instructional practices learned through the Four-Blocks activities transfer into other content areas to improve teaching and learning as well. The framework usually helps teachers and administrators grow through discussion and planning with school personnel, as well as between and among teachers and schools already using the Four Blocks. Most schools find that the Four-Blocks framework affects more than just reading, writing, and word knowledge; it affects classroom behavior and the content areas, while empowering good teachers to become even better.

Here are some tips for administrators in Four-Blocks schools:

- Observe regularly in classrooms and focus on the positive things you see. The first (and probably the best) thing administrators can do is to affirm what teachers do well—and every teacher has some strengths. An observation checklist for each of the activities is included in this book. Once you have gained the trust of the teacher, then constructive feedback can be used. Help your faculty to help each other. Some teachers need help as they try new activities throughout the year. Principals can arrange for teachers to observe each other, to plan together, and to talk about what they are doing and why.

- Arrange a school schedule supportive of the model. Most teachers can fit the Four Blocks into their daily schedules. They decide what works best at what times, which block should be done first, and which block can be done later in the day. When there are too many interruptions in the daily schedule, teachers have difficulty getting to all four blocks.

- Participate in staff development along with your teachers. Teachers know an administrator considers something truly important when that administrator participates with them in a staff development training session.

- Take a Four-Blocks field trip in your school or to another school. The administrator or Four-Blocks leader, along with the teachers as a whole or by grade levels, "tour" the building as if going on a field trip. The "leader" selects rooms to tour based on areas to celebrate or discuss. Sometimes print support is the focus—looking at word walls and theme boards. Sometimes Guided Reading lessons are the focus. The field trip allows the leader to celebrate what's happening in the rooms (What to do!) or helps him or her focus the group on specific concerns (What not to do!). Some schools even use a "Four-Blocks Walk Through" document duplicated to give the teachers a brief glimpse of what to look for when touring the school or classroom.

- "Put your money where your mouth is!" Successful administrators support teachers by making available whatever funds they can find to provide basic materials to make the framework work. Teachers know administrators value the model when they see scarce resources being spent to support it.

- Be a cheerleader for Four Blocks and your teachers! Teachers get little positive feedback about what they are doing and what their school is doing. Once some parts of the Four-Blocks framework are in place and working well, invite visitors to your school. Brag on your teachers' accomplishments and show off what they are doing well. Do be discriminating in what you show off, however. If you have a teacher who is not doing a block well, make sure you don't ever schedule visitors to observe that teacher doing that block. Teachers will soon realize you know and appreciate who is doing what well, and they will be motivated to do more well. Just as with children, success is the key to motivation!

Essential Materials

There are many materials to support Four Blocks. These are the ones we consider most essential*:

- *The Teacher's Guide to the Four Blocks®*
- *Month-by-Month Phonics* series (choose the appropriate grade level)
- Books and magazines (classroom library, books from the school and local library) for Self-Selected Reading
- Multiple copies of grade level and easier texts or anthologies, or sets of books; big books for Guided Reading
- Pocket chart
- Sentence strips
- Index cards
- Word wall or materials to make one
- Making Words cards or materials to make them (clasp envelopes and index cards)
- Individual letter cards for each student
- Handwriting paper (half sheet for word wall practice)
- Red pens or correcting pencils
- Overhead projector (and transparencies) or large lined and unlined chart paper
- Chalkboard or dry erase board (especially if no overhead)
- Add-on editor's checklist
    * Helpful but not essential: Making Words holders; microphone for sharing; phonics phones; beach ball; "author's chair" or "share chair."

Some Topics Teachers Find Helpful for Workshops Once They Know the Basics

- What is Guided Reading the Four-Blocks way? (Some teachers suggest a KWL chart for this workshop. The **K** and **W** are done at the beginning. What do you **Know** about Guided Reading—what do you think it is? The **W** stands for what you **Want** to learn—hopefully how to do Guided Reading the Four-Blocks way! Then, at the end of the workshop—the **L** stands for what teachers have **Learned**.)
- Why is Self-Selected Reading important to a balanced literacy program?
- How do teachers plan Guided Reading lessons with appropriate before-, during-, and after-reading activities?

- How do teachers know what to teach during Guided Reading?
- How do teachers know what to teach during writing mini-lessons?
- How do teachers coach writing during the writing mini-lesson?
- How do teachers choose appropriate books to read aloud to primary students?
- How can teachers support and help each other as they grow and learn?
- How can teachers make connections between the blocks as they plan for instruction daily?
- How do schools use the Four-Blocks framework to teach their curriculum?
- How do Four-Blocks teachers publish student writing?
- How do teachers grade in each of the blocks? *or* What does a school assess and how? (We cannot do this for you; you will have to decide upon this one because expectations differ from school to school and state to state.)
- How do teachers plan a day in the Four-Blocks framework?

Want to Learn Even More About the Four Blocks?

Some good resources for reading, workshops, and study groups are:

- Chapters from *The Teacher's Guide to the Four Blocks®* by Cunningham, Hall, and Sigmon (Carson-Dellosa, 1999) and the video, *The Four-Blocks® Literacy Model: How and Why It Really Works* with Pat Cunningham (Carson-Dellosa, 2001)—to get the picture of what to do and for how long.
- *Month-by-Month Phonics for First Grade* by Cunningham and Hall; *Month-by-Month Phonics for Second Grade* by Hall and Cunningham; and *Month-by-Month Phonics for Third Grade* by Cunningham and Hall (Carson-Dellosa, 1997 and 1998). Teachers are grouped by grade level to study the Working with Words Block and which activities are appropriate for which grade level. Many schools and presenters are now presenting this as a workshop by dividing the teachers into grade-level groups, showing the grade-level *Working with Words* videos with Pat Cunningham (Carson-Dellosa, 2002), and then discussing what they are doing and why.
- *Classrooms That Work, 3rd edition* by Pat Cunningham and Richard Allington (Allyn and Bacon, 2002)—to see the big picture.
- *Phonics They Use, 3rd edition* by Pat Cunningham (Addison-Wesley, 1999)—to see the big picture for Working with Words.
- *Guided Reading the Four-Blocks® Way* by P. Cunningham, Hall, and J. Cunningham (Carson-Dellosa, 2000)—to learn more about teaching reading and reading skills and strategies. Many schools also use the *Guided Reading* video series with Pat Cunningham and Dottie Hall (Carson-Dellosa, 2002).
- *Self-Selected Reading the Four-Blocks® Way* by Cunningham, Hall, and Gambrell (Carson-Dellosa, 2002)—to learn more about that block.
- *Writing Mini-Lessons for First Grade* by Hall, Cunningham, and Boger (Carson-Dellosa, 2002); *Writing Mini-Lessons for Second Grade* by Hall, Cunningham, and Smith (Carson-Dellosa, 2002); and *Writing Mini-Lessons for Third Grade* by Sigmon and Ford (Carson-Dellosa, 2002). Teachers can be grouped by grade levels to study these grade-level appropriate lessons.

Outline of Self-Selected Reading

Goals of the Self-Selected Reading Block

- To introduce children to all types of literature through the teacher read-aloud
- To encourage children's reading interests
- To provide instructional-level reading
- To build intrinsic motivation for reading

Teacher Read-Aloud (5-10 minutes)

The teacher chooses a book(s) and/or selection(s) and reads aloud to all students, including a variety of levels, genres, and authors.

Children Read (15-20 minutes)

Students choose books or magazines at their own level and read independently. (In early first grade, some children may be picture reading or "pretend reading" familiar stories.)

The teacher conferences with individual children in the class. This conference is "child-directed." The child chooses one or two pages to read aloud to the teacher (more pages in first grade if there are only a few words on each page). The teacher and child have a conversation (not an interrogation!) about the book. The teacher asks child-centered questions such as, "What was your favorite part?" or "Why did you choose this book?"

The teacher notes on the child's record sheet the title of the book read and some indication about how fluent the reading was. Other notes may be made to help the teacher document the child's growth in reading and reading interests.

Sometimes, the teacher and child discuss their reading plans for the next week. The teacher may help the struggling readers select books they can and would like to read. The teacher often suggests "challenging" books to advanced readers.

Sharing (Optional) (5-10 minutes)

Students briefly share what they have read. This may occur in different ways: "reader's chair" format with whole class, table sharing or "four square share," buddy sharing, etc.

Total Time for Self-Selected Reading: 30-40 Minutes

Administrator's Checklist for Observing Self-Selected Reading

Name_____ Grade_____ Date_____

What to Look for in Self-Selected Reading

	NO	NI	S	O
The teacher reads aloud expressively.				
The teacher models how he/she gains enjoyment or information from reading.				
The teacher has available a wide variety of materials of different types and on different levels, including easy and challenging books.				
Reading materials are easily accessible, and children do not have to wander to get them.				
Children move into their reading quickly and stay engaged.				
Early in the year, the teacher circulates and encourages the children in their reading. As the year progresses, the teacher conferences with individual children about their reading.				
Once conferencing begins, the teacher has a schedule for conferences, and children know when they have a conference.				
The teacher has spread his/her struggling readers across the days and spends a little more time with the one scheduled for today.				
The teacher has spread out conferences for advanced readers across the days.				
The teacher conducts each conference so that it is more like a "conversation" than an "interrogation."				
The teacher records the book and indicates how well the child read and understood the book.				
Sharing books is optional and might be included at the end of this block. The sharing time should be brief and briskly paced.				
Good classroom management and organization are evident.				
Pacing is appropriate and the block is completed in 30-40 minutes.				

NO = Not Observed; NI = Needs Improvement; S = Satisfactory; O = Outstanding

Comments: _____

_____

_____

Teacher's Self-Evaluation for Self-Selected Reading

Here are some questions to ask yourself to determine how well you are doing Self-Selected Reading and to help you grow in this block.

_____ 1. Am I reading a variety of different kinds of literature—stories, informational books, mysteries, biographies, old favorites, chapter books, poetry, etc.?

_____ 2. Am I including some "quick reads" from magazines, newspapers, encyclopedias, Web sites, and other sources to show children that people read more than just books?

_____ 3. Am I reading materials at different levels—some at grade level; some above grade level; some "easy" books—to model that all levels of books are acceptable?

_____ 4. Am I reading expressively and in an excited manner—stopping and commenting on things I particularly like or find fascinating and modeling daily the pleasure I get from reading?

_____ 5. Have I gathered the widest amount and variety of materials for my children to select from, using school and public library sources if necessary to have what I need?

_____ 6. Do I have interesting easy books and some "challenging" books so that all my children can find something on their level that they want to read?

_____ 7. Are the books easily accessible to children so that they don't have to wander from place to place to get books and waste reading time?

_____ 8. Do children move quickly into their reading, and do they stay engaged?

_____ 9. Early in the year, do I circulate and encourage children in their reading?

_____ 10. As the year progresses, do I conference with a portion of my students daily (often one-fifth of the class each day—fewer if an unusually large class; more often if an unusually small class)?

_____ 11. Have I spread out my struggling readers across the days, and am I giving them a little extra time to "ooh" and "aah" about their reading, as well as helping them choose books they can read and will enjoy?

_____ 12. Have I spread out my advanced readers across the days, and do I occasionally suggest to them a more challenging book I think they can handle and will enjoy?

_____ 13. Do I have conversations (rather than interrogations!) with my children, and do they look forward to their "one-to-one" book talk time with me?

The Administrator's Guide to the Four Blocks®

____ 14. Do I make a record of the book the child chose to conference on and indicate how well the child read and understood this book?

____ 15. Do I provide time for occasional sharing and set up the sharing so that the children and I enjoy it, and it motivates children to expand their reading interests?

____ 16. Have I chosen some of my read-aloud materials, as well as some of the materials available for the children to read, and connected these to my science and social studies topics?

____ 17. Have I paced this block so that it is completed in 30-40 minutes?

A Sample Week for Self-Selected Reading
Early in the Year in First Grade

The teacher read-aloud may include one, two, or three books or selections, depending on the length of books or selections and time allotted.

Monday

Teacher read-aloud: *The Gingerbread Man* by Alan Trussell-Cullen (Dominie Press, Inc., 1999)

The teacher then shares how children could pretend read the book—if they couldn't read all the words, they could remember the story and retell the story.

Children read (or pretend read) for 5-10 minutes. The teacher circulates and encourages.

A few children sharing (optional)

Tuesday

Teacher read-aloud: *ABC I Like Me!* by Nancy Carlson (Viking, 1997)

The teacher then shares how children could pretend read the book—if they couldn't read all the words, they could look at the pictures and "read" the pictures.

Children read (or pretend read) for 5-10 minutes. The teacher circulates and encourages.

A few children sharing (optional)

Wednesday

Teacher read-aloud: *Over in the Meadow* by Jane Cabrera (Holiday House Publishers, 1999)

The teacher then shares how students could pretend read the book—if they couldn't read all the words, they could look at the pictures and "read" the pictures.

Children read (or pretend read) for 5-10 minutes. The teacher circulates and encourages.

A few children sharing (optional)

Thursday

Teacher read-aloud: *Billy and the Big New School* by Catherine and Laurence Anholt (Albert Whitman Co., 1997)

The teacher then shares how children could pretend read the book—if they couldn't read all the words, they could look at the pictures and "read" the pictures.

Children read (or pretend read) for 5-10 minutes. The teacher circulates and encourages.

A few children sharing (optional)

Friday

Teacher read-aloud: *When I Was Little* by Jamie Lee Curtis (HarperCollins, 1993)

The teacher then shares how students could pretend read the book—if they couldn't read all the words, they could look at the pictures and "read" the pictures.

Children read (or pretend read) for 5-10 minutes. The teacher circulates and encourages.

A few children sharing (optional)

A Sample Week for Self-Selected Reading
Later in the Year in First Grade

The teacher read-aloud may include one, two, or three books or selections, depending on the length of books or selections and time allotted.

Monday

Teacher read-aloud: *Animals in the Summer* by Jane McCauley (National Geographic Society, 1988)

The teacher talks about what she read in this book and links it to what the class is learning about animals, reminding the children of the books about animals in the book baskets.

Children read a book (or picture-read the pictures in an animal book) for 15-20 minutes.

Teacher conferences with scheduled children.

A few children sharing (optional)

Tuesday

Teacher read-aloud: *Pigs* by Gail Gibbons (Holiday House Publishers, 1999)

The teacher talks about what she read in this book and links it to what the class is learning about animals.

Children read a book (or picture-read the pictures in an informational book) for 15-20 minutes.

Teacher conferences with scheduled children.

A few children sharing (optional)

Wednesday

Teacher read-aloud: *Click, Clack, Moo: Cows That Type* by Doreen Cronin (Simon and Schuster, 2000)

The teacher asks students if the book could have really happened or if it is fiction (make-believe).

Children read for 15-20 minutes.

The teacher conferences with scheduled children.

A few children sharing (optional)

Thursday

Teacher read-aloud: Chapter 1 of *Junie B., First Grader (At Last!)* by Barbara Park (Random House, 2001)

The teacher talks about this "chapter" book and how she will read a chapter each day. "What will happen in our book tomorrow? I think tomorrow . . . ."

Then, the teacher reads the *Time for Kids* article, "Welcome Baby Panda" (Vol. 5, No. 2).

The teacher talks about the size of pandas compared to other bears.

Children read for 15-20 minutes.

The teacher conferences with scheduled children.

A few children sharing (optional)

Friday

Teacher read-aloud: Chapter 2 of *Junie B., First Grader (At Last!)*

The teacher models how she remembers what she read yesterday and what she predicted the book would be about today. She asks, "What do you think will happen in the next chapter?" and takes a few answers.

Children read for 15-20 minutes.

The teacher conferences with scheduled children.

A few children sharing (optional)

A Sample Week for Self-Selected Reading
Second Grade

The teacher read-aloud may include one, two, or three books or selections, depending on the length of books or selections and time allotted.

Monday

Teacher read-aloud: Chapter 1 in *Donovan's Word Jar* by Monalisa DeGross (HarperTrophy, 1994)

This is an easy chapter book. The teacher talks about today's selection in the "chapter" book, then thinks aloud about tomorrow's chapter: "I think that tomorrow . . . ."

Then, the teacher reads *I Like Jam* by Stella Yang (Rigby, 2001), an easy book, also called an "everyone" book.

Children read for 15-20 minutes.

The teacher conferences with scheduled children.

Children sharing (optional)

Tuesday

Teacher read-aloud: Chapter 2 in *Donovan's Word Jar*

Then, the teacher reads *Kids in the Kitchen* by Jill Eggleton (Rigby, 1999).

Children read for 15-20 minutes.

The teacher conferences with scheduled children.

Children sharing (optional)

Wednesday

Teacher read-aloud: Chapter 3 in *Donovan's Word Jar*

Then, the teacher reads *Weather in the City* by George Wong (National Geographic Society, 2001), an "everyone" book about the science theme, weather.

Children read for 15-20 minutes.

The teacher conferences with scheduled children.

Children sharing (optional)

Thursday

Teacher read-aloud: Chapter 4 in *Donovan's Word Jar*

Then, the teacher reads *Weather Today* by Marvin Buckley (National Geographic Society, 2001), another "everyone" book.

Children read for 15-20 minutes.

Teacher conferences with scheduled children.

Children sharing (optional)

Friday

Teacher read-aloud: Chapter 5 in *Donovan's Word Jar*

The teacher asks, "What do you think will happen in the next chapter?" and takes a few answers.

Then, the teacher reads a *Time for Kids* article on weather in Alaska ("The Big Chill," Vol. 4, No. 17).

Children read for 15-20 minutes.

The teacher conferences with scheduled children.

Children sharing (optional)

A Sample Week for Self-Selected Reading
Third Grade

The teacher read-aloud may include one, two, or three books or selections, depending on the length of books or selections and time allotted.

Monday

Teacher read-aloud: *Mufaro's Beautiful Daughter* by John Steptoe (Scholastic, Inc., 1987)

Then, the teacher reads the one-page introduction, "Who Turned Out the Lights?" from *Understanding Electricity* by Stephen M. Tomecek (National Geographic Society, 2002).

The teacher links the topic to what is being studied in science.

Children read for 15-20 minutes.

The teacher conferences with scheduled children.

Children sharing (optional)

Tuesday

Teacher read-aloud: *The True Story of the Three Pigs* by Jon Scieszka (Scholastic, Inc., 1989)

Then, the teacher reads Chapter 1: Going with the Flow, from *Understanding Electricity*.

Children read for 15-20 minutes.

The teacher conferences with scheduled children.

Children sharing (optional)

Wednesday

Teacher read-aloud: Chapter 1 of *Third Grade Stinks!* by Colleen O'Shaughnessy McKenna (Holiday House Publishers, 2001).

Then, the teacher reads Chapter 2: Power to the People, from *Understanding Electricity*.

Children read for 15-20 minutes.

The teacher conferences with scheduled children.

Children sharing (optional)

Thursday

Teacher read-aloud: Chapter 2 of *Third Grade Stinks!*

Then, the teacher reads Chapter 3: Fueling the Next Generation, from *Understanding Electricity*.

Children read for 15-20 minutes.

The teacher conferences with scheduled children.

Children sharing (optional)

Friday

Teacher read-aloud: Chapter 3 of *Third Grade Stinks!*

Children read for 15-20 minutes.

Teacher conferences with scheduled children.

Children sharing (optional)

CAUTION! THIS BLOCK
UNDER CONSTRUCTION!

Common Roadblocks in Self-Selected Reading

It's not Four Blocks if you are not doing ALL four blocks every single day.
(Well, to be honest, almost every single day!)

It's NOT Self-Selected Reading if you are not reading aloud to students every day.

It's NOT Self-Selected Reading if children are not getting a weekly one-to-one conference.
Self-Selected Reading is not the same as Sustained Silent Reading or Drop Everything and Read. In Self-Selected Reading, the teacher conferences daily with some students while everyone reads.

It's NOT Self-Selected Reading if the conferences consist solely of asking everyone the same questions. Conferences are conversations—not interrogations!

It's NOT Self-Selected Reading if the children are not choosing their own books.
Sometimes Four-Blocks teachers help students select books they can read and will enjoy but teachers do NOT assign books or insist students read only books on a narrow reading level. During Self-Selected Reading conferences, teachers help children choose books they can read and will enjoy. Self-Selected Reading cannot be multilevel if there is not a range of books to interest all children or books for all levels in the classroom.

Clever Four-Blocks teachers gradually increase the amount of time the children read, starting with 5-10 minutes and building up to 15-20 minutes.

Outline of Guided Reading

Goals of the Guided Reading Block

- To teach comprehension skills and strategies
- To develop background knowledge, meaning vocabulary, and oral language
- To teach children how to read all types of literature
- To provide as much instructional-level reading as possible
- To maintain the motivation and self-confidence of struggling readers

Before Reading (5-15 minutes)

The teacher introduces and supports text with the whole group of students by preparing them to read the chosen text. Before-reading preparation may include:

- Activating and building students' prior knowledge about the text and topic.
- Introducing and discussing key vocabulary words for the selection.
- Modeling a think-aloud ("This reminds me of . . ." or "I wonder why . . .").
- Starting a KWL chart or other graphic organizer (informational text).
- Starting a story map or reviewing the Beach Ball questions (story or fiction).
- Previewing the book or text and making predictions ("I wonder if . . .").
- Setting a clear purpose for reading ("After we read, we will all come back together and . . . Be sure you read so you can help us . . .").
- Focusing on a particular comprehension strategy (connect, predict/anticipate, summarize/conclude, question/monitor, image/infer, evaluate/apply, etc.).

During Reading (15-20 minutes)

Through a variety of flexible grouping formats, the teacher provides support for all students to read the text that has been introduced. Grouping may be paired or Playschool Groups, Three-Ring Circus (some children reading individually, some partner reading, and the teacher reading with a group of children or a child who needs special assistance), whole group (Echo or Choral Reading, Shared Reading, ERT . . .), Book Club Groups/Literature Circles, etc.

The teacher chooses a support role during the reading: actively involved in reading with whole group, small group; taking anecdotal notes as individual students read; or monitoring the partners/groups as they read and coaching where needed.

After Reading (10-15 minutes)

Whatever purpose was set for reading is immediately followed up on after reading. Activities involve the whole class and may include:

- Following up a strategy introduced before reading.
- Completing a story map or doing the Beach Ball.
- Acting out the story or "doing the book."
- Completing a graphic organizer or KWL chart.
- Drawing, writing, or discussing as a response to reading.

Total Time for Guided Reading: 30-45 Minutes

Administrator's Checklist for Observing Guided Reading

Name_____ Grade_____ Date_____

What to Look for in Guided Reading

	NO	NI	S	O
Before reading, the teacher helps children access and build prior knowledge, including meaning vocabulary on some days.				
The teacher sets a clear purpose for reading so that children know why they are reading and what they will do after reading.				
During reading, the teacher chooses a format (partners, Three-Ring Circus, Book Club group, Shared Reading, etc.) that provides the support necessary for all children to succeed in reading the text.				
The children move quickly into the format and know what is expected of them during reading.				
While the children read, the teacher uses his/her time to monitor, assess, and coach children in ways appropriate to the format.				
The teacher sets reasonable time limits for reading and makes it clear to students what to do if they finish reading before the time is up.				
After reading, the teacher follows up the purpose set for reading.				
The after-reading activity focuses on comprehension and helps children learn how to think as they read.				
Good classroom management and organization are evident.				
Pacing is appropriate and the block is completed in 30-45 minutes.				

NO = Not Observed; NI = Needs Improvement; S = Satisfactory; O = Outstanding

Comments: _____

_____

_____

_____

_____

_____

_____

_____

The Administrator's Guide to the Four Blocks®   © Carson-Dellosa CD-2425

Teacher's Self-Evaluation for Guided Reading

Here are some questions to ask yourself to determine how well you are doing Guided Reading and to help you grow in this block.

_____ 1. Am I including a variety of different kinds of literature—stories, informational books, mysteries, biographies, old favorites, chapter books, poetry, plays, etc.?

_____ 2. Am I including grade-level and easier materials?

_____ 3. Am I using a variety of activities to prepare children before they read?

_____ 4. Am I helping children access and build prior knowledge and important meaning vocabulary?

_____ 5. Am I setting a clear purpose for reading so that children know exactly what they will do after reading and will read to get ready to do that?

_____ 6. Am I using a variety of during-reading formats to provide the support necessary for all my children to succeed in reading the text for the purpose I set?

_____ 7. Am I modeling and role-playing the formats (partner reading, Book Club Groups, etc.) so that my children know exactly what is expected of them?

_____ 8. Am I using my time while the children read to monitor, assess, and coach children in ways appropriate to the format I am using?

_____ 9. Do I set and stick to reasonable time limits for children's reading and make it clear to them what to do if they finish reading before the time is up?

_____ 10. Do I immediately follow up the purpose I set for reading so that my children "take me seriously" when I tell them what they need to be ready to do after we read?

_____ 11. Does my after-reading activity focus on comprehension and help children learn how we think as we read?

_____ 12. Do I seek out or create materials students can read during Guided Reading which connect to my science and social studies topics?

_____ 13. Am I pacing this block so that it is completed in 30-45 minutes?

A Sample Week for Guided Reading Early in the Year in First Grade

Some weeks, early in the year, the teacher may spend all week reading and rereading two big books. Other weeks, multiple copies of small books or basal readers may be used.

Monday

Big Book: *See What I Can Do!* by Mary E. Pearson (Steck-Vaughn Co., 2002)

Before: This book is predictable by pictures. The teacher takes a picture walk through the book and talks about how the pictures will help with the new vocabulary words in this book: tie shoe, paint picture, brush teeth, brush hair, write name, swing high, stack blocks, button jacket, ride tricycle, put puzzle together, pour milk, work on computer, put away toys, jump rope, and read book.

During: Shared Reading—For the first reading, the teacher reads the story to the class. The book is read again and the children join in and share the reading.

After: The teacher discusses what the children in this book can do. She asks students, "What can you do?"

Tuesday

Big Book: *See What I Can Do!*

Before: The teacher talks about all the things the children in this book can do. Then, the teacher makes a list, writing each item on sentence strips, and reads the book again to see if the list is complete.

During: Choral Reading—The teacher reads the first line, "See what I can do!" and the children read the second line, using the picture for a prompt. The format repeats for each page with the teacher reading the first line and the children reading the second.

After: Each child finishes this sentence, "I can _____," then he draws a picture to illustrate what he can do. The teacher makes a class book with the children's responses.

Wednesday

Big Book: *Little? I'm Just the Right Size!* by Mary E. Pearson (Steck-Vaughn Co., 2002)

Before: The teacher takes a picture walk through this big book, talking about what is happening in the pictures and letting the pictures help with some words if needed.

During: Shared Reading—For the first reading, the teacher reads the story to the class. The book is read again and the children join in and "share the reading."

After: The teacher tosses the Beach Ball and lets the child who catches it answer one of the questions on the ball. This continues as time allows.

Thursday

Big Book: *Little? I'm Just the Right Size!*

Before: The teacher talks about the story she read yesterday and fills in a story map, then reads the book again to see if the story map is correct.

During: Echo Reading—The class reads each page after the teacher.

After: The teacher and the class read the book again while some children act out the story ("doing the book").

Friday

Big Books: *See What I Can Do!* and *Little? I'm Just the Right Size!*

Before: The teacher talks about the two books read this week. She asks, "Which book is real? Which book is make-believe? What did you like about each book?" The class votes on their favorite book.

During: The teacher and children read the favorite book again, together.

After: Each child finishes the sentence, "My favorite book was _____." Then, she illustrates the sentence with her favorite big book this week.

A Sample Week for Guided Reading
Later in the Year in First Grade

Each week the class reads "grade level" and "easier" selections. The shared reading of a big book is always an "easier" selection.

Monday

Book: *If You Give a Mouse a Cookie* by Laura Numeroff, illustrated by Felicia Bond (HarperCollins, 1985)

Before: The teacher talks about the title, author, and illustrator, then takes a picture walk through the book, making predictions about what will happen.

During: Partner Reading—The students read the book with partners, then talk about the predictions.

After: Discussion—The teacher asks, "Were the predictions right? Which were? Which were not?"

Tuesday

Book: *If You Give a Mouse a Cookie*

Before: The teacher talks about what happened in this story and asks the class if they think this could really happen. The teacher has the children read the story again and be ready to answer that question.

During: Playschool Groups—The students read in groups of four or five with a "teacher" leader.

After: The teacher, with the help of the class, makes a list of what could be true and what could not happen. If there is time, the students draw something that could not happen in real life.

Wednesday

Book: *If You Give a Mouse a Cookie*

Before: The teacher talks about all of the things the mouse might want in the order they happened in this story. The teacher has the children read to see if the list and sequence are correct.

During: Three-Ring Circus—Some students read by themselves, some read with a partner, and some read with the teacher.

After: The teacher checks the list and sequence, making any changes the class wants to make after reading and checking.

Thursday

Big Book: *The Scrubbing Machine* by Joy Cowley (Wright Group, 1998)

Before: The teacher asks, "What is a scrubbing machine? He takes a picture walk through the book, naming some of the things the machine is scrubbing and finding those words in the text. The teacher has the children read to find out all of the things the machine scrubbed.

During: Shared Reading—The teacher reads the big book to the students, then reads it again, asking the children to join in and share the reading, using the pictures to help them if needed.

After: The teacher asks, "What did the machine scrub?" He and the class name and discuss all of the things scrubbed.

Friday

Big Book: *The Scrubbing Machine*

Before: The teacher talks with the students about the following story elements: character, setting, beginning, middle, and end. He tells the students that after reading, they will answer the Beach Ball questions related to these story elements.

During: The teacher reads two pages, then the children read the two pages with repetitive print. The teacher reminds the children to use the pictures and print to help.

After: The teacher tosses the Beach Ball and lets the child who catches it answer one of the questions on the ball. This continues as time allows.

A Sample Week for Guided Reading
Second Grade

Monday

Book: *Henry and Mudge: The First Book* by Cynthia Rylant (Simon and Schuster, 1996)

Before: The teacher talks about other books by Cynthia Rylant, including *The Relatives Came*. She leads the class in Rivet with vocabulary from the book: Henry, Mudge, different, hundred, parents, searched, and weighed. She asks the children to predict what this story will be about from these words.

During: ERT . . . Everyone reads to find out if the predictions are correct by reading the first chapter of *Henry and Mudge: The First Book*.

After: The class discusses their predictions. The teacher asks, "Did any of your predictions really happen?" She leads the class as they make new oral sentences that did really happen using vocabulary from the Rivet activity.

Tuesday

Book: *Henry and Mudge: The First Book*

Before: The teacher reviews what the class found out about Henry yesterday. She asks, "What did he want? What did he get?"

During: ERT . . . The class reads the second chapter of the book, Mudge. Everyone reads to find out and figure out about Mudge, the dog.

After: The teacher asks, "What kind of dog did Henry want? What did he get?" (If there is time, the teacher reads the description of Mudge and has each student draw a picture.)

Wednesday

Book: *Henry and Mudge: The First Book*

Before: The teacher reviews what has happened so far in *Henry and Mudge: The First Book*. In the last chapter, Henry worries about lots of things. The teacher has the students read to find out how Mudge helped Henry stop worrying.

During: Three-Ring Circus—Some students read by themselves, some read with a partner, and some read with the teacher.

After: The teacher and students write about how Mudge helped Henry stop worrying.

Thursday

Book: *Monkey-Monkey's Tricks* by Patricia McKissack (Random House, Inc., 1988) easy book

Before: The teacher talks about folk tales and what is commonly found in folk tales. She leads the class in Rivet with the new vocabulary words from the book: monkey, hyena, giraffe, elephant, creature, monster, bubbling, and boiling. She asks the children to make predictions using the vocabulary words.

During: Playschool Groups—The students read to page 26 in groups of four or five. Each group has a "teacher" leader.

After: The teacher and students discuss the predictions made based on the vocabulary used for Rivet and come up with sentences that really happened using these vocabulary words.

Friday

Book: *Monkey-Monkey's Tricks*

Before: The teacher and students talk about what has happened in the book so far. The teacher has the children read to find out what happens in the middle and how this folk tale ends. She asks students to be ready to answer questions on the Beach Ball.

During: Playschool Groups—The students read pages 27-48 in the same groups from yesterday.

After: The teacher tosses the Beach Ball and lets the child who catches it answer one of the questions on the ball. This continues as time allows.

A Sample Week for Guided Reading
Third Grade

Monday

Book: *Sunken Treasure* by Gail Gibbons (HarperTrophy, 1990)

Before: The teacher and students talk about sunken treasure. The teacher leads the class in Rivet with the new words: *Atocha*, galleon, equipment, exploring, instruments, investigate, propellers, evidence, muskets, precious. He asks the students to predict what this book is about based on these new vocabulary words.

During: ERT . . . Everyone reads pages 1-17 to find out (or figure out) whether or not the predictions are correct.

After: The teacher follows up the predictions made based on the vocabulary words used for Rivet. Using these words, the children come up with new sentences that actually happened.

Tuesday

Book: *Sunken Treasure*

Before: The teacher reviews what has been read so far—how the *Atocha* sunk and why Spain searched for it. The teacher asks the students to predict if the ship was salvaged and the treasure recovered.

During: ERT . . . Everyone reads pages 18-28 to find out whether the predictions are correct.

After: Each student writes a paragraph to tell how the crew recorded, salvaged, and restored the treasure from the salvage site.

Wednesday

Book: *Sunken Treasure*

Before: The teacher reviews what the students have learned so far about the *Atocha* and what the crew did when they found the ship. The remaining pages of the book describe four other ships that sank. Begin a data chart with the names of these four ships and columns to record information (when and how the ship sank, when and how the ship was found, how the ship was salvaged, and what was learned about the past from the salvaged ship).

During: Partner Reading—Students read with partners to get the information for the data chart.

After: The teacher and students complete the data chart and discuss when and how each ship sank, when and how each ship was found, how each ship was salvaged, and what was learned about the past from each of the salvaged ships.

Thursday

Book Club Groups—four books with approximately six copies of each book

1. *The Titanic Lost . . . and Found* by Judy Donnelly (Random House, 1987) easy

2. *Titanic* by Victoria Shaw (Scholastic, Inc., 1999) average

3. *Tonight on the Titanic* by Mary Pope Osborne (Random House, 1999) average

4. *Polar the Titanic Bear* by Daisy Cronin Stone Spedder (Little, Brown and Co., 1994) harder

The Administrator's Guide to the Four Blocks®

Before: The teacher shows and gives a book talk on each of the four books.

During: Book Club Groups—In four groups, the children preview the books to find and make first, second, and third choices of the book they would like to read.

After: The teacher has children list their first, second, and third choices for the book they want to read. The students come back together as a big group and turn in their choices to the teacher, who explains what will happen tomorrow with their Book Club Groups.

Friday

Book Club Groups: Four books on *Titanic: The Titanic Lost . . . and Found* by Judy Donnelly (easy); *Titanic* by Victoria Shaw (average); *Tonight on the Titanic* by Mary Pope Osborne (average); *Polar the Titanic Bear* by Daisy Cronin Stone Spedder (harder).

Before: The teacher assigns children to their Book Club Groups based on their choices from Thursday. She points out that not everyone got their first choice, but everyone got one of their three choices. She talks about some *Titanic*-related words they may come across when reading today. She tells students that they will read the first third of their books and begin story maps by filling in the characters, setting, and what happened in the beginning of their books.

During: Students read the first third of their books in Book Club Groups.

After: Each group tells about their book's characters and setting, as well as what happens at the beginning of the book. The groups compare how the different books begin to tell the same story.

CAUTION! THIS BLOCK
UNDER CONSTRUCTION!
Common Roadblocks in Guided Reading

It's not Four Blocks if you are not doing ALL four blocks every single day.
(Well, to be honest, almost every single day!)

It's NOT Four Blocks if children are grouped according to reading level during the Guided Reading Block!

It's NOT Four Blocks if the focus is on words instead of comprehension during the Guided Reading Block.

Four-Blocks teachers work with words during the Working with Words Block and remind children to use what they are learning as they read during Guided Reading. The focus of the Guided Reading Block is comprehension!

It's NOT Four Blocks if children are reading during Guided Reading in a whole group—round-robin style.

Four-Blocks teachers use lots of different formats on different days during Guided Reading (Shared Reading, Echo Reading, ERT . . ., Partner Reading, Three-Ring Circus, Book Club Groups, etc.).

It's NOT Four Blocks if there are not daily before-, during-, and after-reading activities during Guided Reading.

Outline of Writing

Goals of the Writing Block

- To have students view writing as a way of telling about things
- To develop fluent writing for all children
- To teach students to use grammar and mechanics in their own writing
- To teach particular writing forms
- To allow students to learn to read through writing
- To maintain the motivation and self-confidence of struggling writers

Mini-Lesson (5-10 minutes)

The teacher models writing, showing children how to do all the complex things writers must do. Each mini-lesson has a particular focus which varies with grade level, time of year, and the needs of children. Some examples of mini-lesson focuses include:

- Modeling how to write using think-alouds.
- Modeling how to write a good sentence (or paragraph).
- Writing is telling about something.
- What to do about spelling.
- Choosing a topic.
- Adding on to a piece.
- Using an editor's checklist (adding on to an editor's checklist).
- Procedures for publishing.
- How to write a particular form (story, report, letter, etc.).

Writing (15-20 minutes)

The students write. Some children are beginning a new piece; others are continuing to work on a piece that takes several days to write. Some children, who have conferenced with the teacher, are editing or publishing. Children are at all different stages of the writing process.

The teacher conferences with individuals or small groups of children. Early in the year, these conferences are to "ooh" and "aah" about students' writing and encourage the children at whatever level of writing they are. As the year continues, the conferences usually focus on helping children revise, edit, and publish.

Author's Chair (5-10 minutes)

Children share their writing with each other. In most classrooms, one-fifth of the children share each day, reading one piece they have written since their last sharing day. Children share published pieces, first drafts, or "works in progress." After each child shares his or her writing, several children are invited to make "nice" comments and/or ask a question.

Total Time for Writing: 30-45 Minutes

Administrator's Checklist for Observing Writing

Name_____ Grade_____ Date_____

What to Look for in Writing

	NO	NI	S	O
The teacher gathers the children together for a mini-lesson.				
In the mini-lesson, the teacher models writing, showing and talking about how writers think as they write.				
The mini-lesson focuses on one thing (choosing a topic, what to do about spelling, capital letters, etc.) which will help the students become better writers.				
The children settle into writing quickly and know what is expected of them during writing.				
Except in focused writing lessons, the teacher lets the children choose their own topics for writing and encourages them to take as many days as needed to write each piece.				
Different children are at different stages of the writing process—completing a first draft, adding on, revising, editing, and publishing.				
Early in the year, the teacher circulates and encourages the children to write. As the year progresses, the teacher conferences with individual children about their writing.				
Once conferencing begins, the teacher has a schedule for conferences, and children know when they are scheduled.				
When publishing a piece, the children use the editor's checklist to edit their own writing and may help each other edit before conferencing and editing with the teacher.				
The Writing Block ends with Author's Chair in which several children share their writing—first draft, published, or in progress.				
Once Author's Chair begins, the teacher has a schedule for sharing, and children know when they are scheduled.				
Good classroom management and organization are evident.				
Pacing is appropriate and the block is completed in 30-45 minutes.				

NO = Not Observed; NI = Needs Improvement; S = Satisfactory; O = Outstanding

Comments: _____

Teacher's Self-Evaluation for Writing

Here are some questions to ask yourself to determine how well you are doing Writing and to help you grow in this block.

_____ 1. Do I gather the children together each day for my mini-lesson, modeling how to write as I write and talking about how I think as I write?

_____ 2. Am I focusing my mini-lesson on the one thing I have chosen to help my children move forward in their writing?

_____ 3. Am I doing several mini-lessons with the same focus so that all my children will learn how to do what I am focusing on?

_____ 4. Am I looking at my students' writing and at our curriculum to decide on appropriate mini-lessons?

_____ 5. Am I letting children choose their own topics for writing and encouraging them to take as many days as needed to write each piece?

_____ 6. Am I using my time while the children are writing to conference with children, encouraging them in their efforts early in the year and helping them revise, edit, and publish as the year goes on?

_____ 7. Am I helping children select some pieces to publish, and not publish everything (even if they want to)?

_____ 8. Am I providing opportunities for children to share what they write with each other and modeling positive comments and thoughtful questions in response to their writing?

_____ 9. As the year goes on, am I including some focused writing lessons in which children learn to write particular forms?

_____ 10. Am I teaching children how to edit their own writing and, as the year goes on, how to peer edit?

_____ 11. Am I including appropriate grammar and mechanics in my mini-lessons and on my editor's checklist, as well as teaching students to apply these in their own writing?

_____ 12. On some days during my mini-lesson, am I writing about science and social studies topics and encouraging my students to do so as well, if they choose?

_____ 13. Have I paced this block so that it is completed in 30-45 minutes?

The Administrator's Guide to the Four Blocks® © Carson-Dellosa CD-2425

A Sample Week for Writing
Early in the Year in First Grade

Monday

Writing Mini-lesson: Writing is telling about something

The teacher tells about the time she slipped on the stairs and hurt her foot. She then writes a sentence or two about it and draws a picture.

Children write: The teacher roams around the room, encouraging and helping children who need it. Children write at least a sentence and draw a picture to go with it.

Children share: The teacher gathers the children, and they show and tell about what they are writing.

Tuesday

Writing Mini-lesson: Expanding a sentence or sentences with questions

The teacher reads the two sentences from yesterday and asks the class what they want to know. She answers those questions, then writes some more sentences and adds to the picture.

Children write: The teacher roams around the room, encouraging and helping children who need it. Children add on to their piece or begin a new piece and draw a picture.

Children share: The teacher gathers the children, and they show and tell about what they are writing.

Wednesday

Writing Mini-lesson: Modeling how to choose a topic

The teacher thinks aloud and writes a list of several things she knows about and could write about.

Children write: The teacher roams around the room, encouraging and helping children as they write and draw.

Children share: The teacher gathers the children, and they show and tell about what they are writing.

Thursday

Writing Mini-lesson: Modeling how to write using think-alouds

The teacher chooses a topic from yesterday's list and begins to write, thinking aloud and talking about what she will write, how she will write it, and why.

Children write: The teacher roams around the room, encouraging and helping children who need it as they write and draw.

Children share: The teacher gathers the children, and they show and tell about what they are writing.

Friday

Writing Mini-lesson: What to do about spelling

The teacher writes and models for the class how she uses the word wall, words in the room, and stretching out words to spell words she does not know when writing.

Children write: The teacher roams around the room, encouraging and helping children as they write and draw.

Children share: The teacher gathers the children, and they show and tell about what they are writing.

A Sample Week for Writing
Later in the Year in First Grade

Monday

Writing Mini-lesson: Writing about a topic the class is studying

The teacher and the class discuss what they have learned about plants in science. They write a piece together about what they know about plants.

Children write: The teacher conferences with children about their writing.

Author's Chair: One-fifth of the children share their writing, either a piece in progress or a finished piece.

Tuesday

Writing Mini-lesson: Writing a story with a beginning, middle, and end

The teacher begins a story about visiting her sister over spring break. She writes the beginning of the story using a think-aloud.

Children write: The teacher conferences with children about their writing.

Author's Chair: One-fifth of the children share their writing, either a piece in progress or a finished piece.

Wednesday

Writing Mini-lesson: Writing a story with a beginning, middle, and end

The teacher reads the beginning of the story about visiting her sister over spring break. She writes the middle of the story using a think-aloud, emphasizing what she does about spelling when writing.

Children write: The teacher conferences with children about their writing.

Author's Chair: One-fifth of the children share their writing, either a piece in progress or a finished piece.

Thursday

Writing Mini-lesson: Writing a story with a beginning, middle, and end

The teacher reads the beginning and middle of the story about visiting her sister over spring break. She writes the end of the story using a think-aloud, emphasizing capital letters and ending punctuation marks.

The Administrator's Guide to the Four Blocks® © Carson-Dellosa CD-2425

Children write: The teacher conferences with children about their writing.

Author's Chair: One-fifth of the children share their writing, either a piece in progress or a finished piece.

Friday

Writing Mini-lesson: Revising and self-editing

The teacher rereads her story and adds a sentence that is needed. Then, she talks about the editor's checklist and checks her story for the items on the checklist.

Children write: The teacher conferences with children about their writing.

Author's Chair: One-fifth of the children share their writing, either a piece in progress or a finished piece.

A Sample Week for Writing
Second Grade

Monday

Writing Mini-lesson: Using a web to organize

The teacher makes a web and writes on the spokes the different things they have learned about weather.

Children write: The teacher conferences with children about their writing.

Author's Chair: One-fifth of the children share their writing, either a piece in progress or a finished piece.

Tuesday

Writing Mini-lesson: Using a web to write

The teacher uses the web from the previous day to organize the informational piece about weather and write two paragraphs about what the students have learned about weather.

Children write: The teacher conferences with children about their writing.

Author's Chair: One-fifth of the children share their writing, either a piece in progress or a finished piece.

Wednesday

Writing Mini-lesson: Adding on to a piece

The teacher reads what she has written so far and adds on to it using the web.

Children write: The teacher conferences with children about their writing.

Author's Chair: One-fifth of the children share their writing, either a piece in progress or a finished piece.

Thursday

Writing Mini-lesson: Editing using an editor's checklist

The teacher reads the piece on weather using the editor's checklist to model how to self-edit a piece.

Children write: The teacher conferences with children about their writing.

Author's Chair: One-fifth of the children share their writing, either a piece in progress or a finished piece.

Friday

Writing Mini-lesson: Writing is telling about something

The teacher talks about the baseball game (play, movie, etc.) she saw last night and writes about it.

Children write: The teacher conferences with children about their writing.

Author's Chair: One-fifth of the children share their writing, either a piece in progress or a finished piece.

A Sample Week for Writing
Third Grade

Monday

Writing Mini-lesson: Writing a thank-you note

The teacher and the children discuss the holiday program the fifth graders just put on. They talk about writing a thank-you note to them. The teacher outlines the format the students should use and models how to write a thank-you note by writing one.

Children write: The teacher conferences with children about their writing.

Author's Chair: One-fifth of the children share their writing, either a piece in progress or a finished piece.

Tuesday

Writing Mini-lesson: Beginning a story: characters and setting

The teacher models how to write the beginning of a story with the character(s) and setting (place and time).

Children write: The teacher conferences with children about their writing.

Author's Chair: One-fifth of the children share their writing, either a piece in progress or a finished piece.

Wednesday

Writing Mini-lesson: A story is not complete without an ending.

The teacher reads what he has written so far, then adds details and an ending.

Children write: The teacher conferences with children about their writing.

Author's Chair: One-fifth of the children share their writing, either a piece in progress or a finished piece.

Thursday

Writing Mini-lesson: Editing with an editor's checklist

The teacher and children use the editor's checklist to edit the teacher's story (see Tuesday and Wednesday).

Children write: The teacher conferences with children about their writing.

Author's Chair: One-fifth of the children share their writing, either a piece in progress or a finished piece.

Friday

Writing Mini-lesson: Writing a personal narrative

The teacher writes about a special day he spent with his grandparents and suggests that children might want to write a personal narrative about a special day they remember.

Children write: The teacher conferences with children about their writing.

Author's Chair: One-fifth of the children share their writing, either a piece in progress or a finished piece.

CAUTION! THIS BLOCK UNDER CONSTRUCTION!

Common Roadblocks in Writing

It's not Four Blocks if you are not doing ALL four blocks every single day.
(Well, to be honest, almost every single day!)

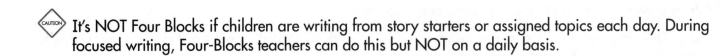

It's NOT Four Blocks if children are writing from story starters or assigned topics each day. During focused writing, Four-Blocks teachers can do this but NOT on a daily basis.

It's NOT Four Blocks if you do not include a daily mini-lesson in which you write for children and model the many things writers think about and do when writing.

In Four-Blocks classrooms, children are not expected to write and spell correctly on a first draft (except for word wall words!). If the piece is to be published, then the student, with help from the teacher, takes the writing through the revision and editing process, at which time spelling errors are fixed.

It's NOT Four Blocks if every piece that is written has to be taken through all the steps of the writing process.

Publishing individual books or class books gives children a reason to revise and edit. Four-Blocks classrooms publish (make public) some student writing.

It's NOT Four Blocks if children don't have a daily sharing time. It is this sharing time that helps many children find topics they know and can write about.

The Administrator's Guide to the Four Blocks®

Outline of Working with Words

Goals of the Working with Words Block

- To teach children how to read and spell high-frequency words

- To teach children how to decode and spell lots of other words using patterns from known words

- To have students automatically and fluently use phonics and spelling patterns while reading and writing (transfer!)

Word Wall (5-15 minutes)

The teacher chooses five words to focus on. On the first day, new words are introduced; on the following day(s), the new words are the words focused on. For the next two or three days, the teacher chooses any five words—including words that need to be reviewed and new words.

The teacher calls out the five words and leads the children in a rhythmic chant of the spelling of these words. Most days, each word is chanted 3-5 times. Next, the children write the words. The teacher models how to write each word—emphasizing correct handwriting. The words are generally written on half sheets of handwriting paper.

After the words are written, the teacher leads the children in checking their papers. Many teachers have the children outline each word with a colored pen—emphasizing the placement of letters above, on, and below the lines.

Early in the year, it takes all the time allotted to word wall to call out, chant, write, and check five words. As the year goes on and the children become faster, teachers often include an On-the-Back activity. Children turn their papers over to the back side and teachers direct children in one of many On-the-Back activities.

Phonics/Spelling Patterns (15-25 minutes)

A variety of activities is used for the second activity in the Working with Words Block. These include but are not limited to:

- Making Words: Children use letters to make dictated words, sort the words for beginning sounds or patterns, and use the patterns to decode and spell new words.

- Rounding Up the Rhymes: The teacher rereads pages of a book with lots of rhymes. The children and teacher "round up the rhymes." These rhyming words are then used to decode and spell new words.

- Reading/Writing Rhymes: The teacher writes a rhyming pattern several times on the chalkboard or on a chart. The teacher distributes beginning letter cards to children who bring to the front a letter or letters that make a real word with the rhyming pattern. After the chart of rhyming words is complete, the teacher and children write silly sentences using the rhyming words.

- Guess the Covered Word: Children use context clues, beginning letters, and word length to guess words in sentences, paragraphs, and big books.

- Using Words You Know: Children use words they know to figure out how to decode and spell other words with the same rhyming pattern.

TOTAL TIME FOR WORKING WITH WORDS: 30-40 MINUTES

Administrator's Checklist for Observing Working with Words

Name_____ Grade_____ Date_____

What to Look for in Working with Words

	NO	NI	S	O
The word wall includes words that are high frequency and/or have useful spelling patterns.				
The words on the word wall are displayed on colorful paper under the letter they begin with. The words are big enough for the children to see and are in a place where everyone can easily see them.				
The teacher does a daily practice in which students chant and write five words, then emphasize handwriting as they write the words.				
Once the children can chant and write the words quickly, the teacher includes an On-the-Back activity, which helps them learn the words and apply the patterns to other words.				
The teacher reminds the children that the word wall is there to support their writing and that they need to spell word wall words correctly in everything they write.				
Following the word wall practice, the teacher leads the children in an activity (Making Words, Rounding Up the Rhymes, Guess the Covered Word, etc.) that helps children learn to decode and spell using patterns.				
The teacher emphasizes the transfer of Working with Words activities to actually decoding words while reading and spelling words while writing. (For example, if a Making Words activity is done, the Make, Sort, and Transfer steps are all included.)				
The teacher keeps a brisk pace while doing Working with Words activities so that students stay engaged and time is available to emphasize transfer.				
A chart of theme, unit, or monthly words is displayed to support children's writing without cluttering up the word wall.				
Pacing is appropriate and the block is completed in 30-40 minutes.				

NO = Not Observed; NI = Needs Improvement; S = Satisfactory; O = Outstanding

Comments: _____

_____

_____

_____

Teacher's Self-Evaluation for Working with Words

Here are some questions to ask yourself to determine how well you are doing Working with Words and to help you grow in this block.

_____ 1. Am I limiting the number of word wall words and including words that are high frequency and/or have useful spelling patterns?

_____ 2. Am I displaying the words on colorful paper, under the letter they begin with, big enough for the children to see and in a place where everyone can easily see them?

_____ 3. Am I doing a daily practice in which the class and I chant and write five words and emphasize handwriting as we write the words?

_____ 4. Once the children can chant and write the words quickly, am I including some On-the-Back activities which help them learn the words and apply the patterns to other words?

_____ 5. Once words are on the word wall, do I hold children accountable for spelling them correctly in everything they write?

_____ 6. Am I including a variety of activities (Making Words, Rounding Up the Rhymes, Guess the Covered Word, etc.) to help children learn to decode and spell using patterns?

_____ 7. Am I emphasizing the transfer of Working with Words activities to actually decoding words while reading and spelling words while writing (for example, including all three steps—make, sort, and transfer—in my Making Words lessons)?

_____ 8. Am I keeping a brisk pace with my Working with Words activities so that I can complete them in 20 minutes, have time to emphasize transfer, and keep the children engaged?

_____ 9. Do I remind children when they are actually reading and writing (during the other three blocks) to use the strategies we practice during Working with Words activities?

_____ 10. On some days, do I connect my Working with Words activities to something read aloud or read during Guided Reading or to my science and social studies topics?

_____ 11. Do I display a chart of theme, unit, or monthly words to support children's writing without cluttering up the word wall?

_____ 12. Am I pacing this block so that it is completed in 30-40 minutes?

A Sample Week for Working with Words
Early in the Year in First Grade

Monday

Word Wall: The teacher adds the following words: can, do, I, see, what. The teacher and students chant, write, and check the new words.

Rounding Up the Rhymes: The teacher uses the rhyming book *I Wish that I Had Duck Feet* by Theo. LeSieg (Random House, 1991) for this activity.

Tuesday

Word Wall: The teacher leads the class in practicing the new words: can, do, I, see, what. The teacher and students chant, write, and check the new words.

Making Words: Make—an at mat sat Pat tap tan ant ants pants

Sort—first letter; rhymes

Transfer—flat rants plan scat

Wednesday

Word Wall: The teacher leads the class in practicing some new and old words: big, can, come, went, what. The teacher and students chant, write, and check the words.

Guess the Covered Word: The teacher writes four to five simple "like-to" sentences with the children's names. She uses what they like to do as the covered word (for example, "Jennifer likes to ☐ .")

Thursday

Word Wall: The teacher leads the class in practicing some new and old words: do, down, fun, went, what. The teacher and students chant, write, and check the words.

Making Words: Make—be Ben ten net bet Bert bent rent Brent

Sort—names; first letter; rhymes

Transfer—flat rants plan scat

Friday

Word Wall: The teacher leads the class in practicing some new and old words: I, in, is, went, what. The teacher and students chant, write, and check the words.

Tongue Twisters: The teacher helps students identify words that begin with certain letters in a tongue twister book. She uses *An Alphabet Book of Cats and Dogs* by Sheila Moxley (Little, Brown and Co., 2001) for this activity.

A Sample Week for Working with Words
Later in the Year in First Grade

Monday

Word Wall: The teacher adds the following words: from, make, night, there, won't. The teacher and students chant, write, and check the new words.

Guess the Covered Word: The teacher writes some sentences related to the science unit on weather for this activity. The science vocabulary words are used as the covered words.

Tuesday

Word Wall: The teacher leads the students in practicing the new words: from, make, night, there, won't. The teacher and students chant, write, and check the new words. On-the-Back activity—Be a Mind Reader with the new words

Rounding Up the Rhymes: The teacher uses the rhyming book *Oh, How I Wished I Could Read!* by John Gile (JGC/United Publishing Corps, 1995) for this activity.

Wednesday

Word Wall: The teacher leads the students in practicing some new and old words: from, for, make, made, where. The teacher and students chant, write, and check the words. On-the-Back activity—words that rhyme with make: cake, bake, snake, flake, quake

Making Words: Make—in win law lawn king wing wink link walk walking

Sort—related words: walk, walking; rhymes

Transfer—sting stink cling slip

Thursday

Word Wall: The teacher leads the students in practicing some new and old words: night, nice, can't, won't, what. The teacher and students chant, write, and check the words. On-the-Back activity—words that rhyme with night: right, fight, bright, fright, light

Reading/Writing Rhymes: The teacher uses the -ing rhyming pattern for this activity.

Friday

Word Wall: The teacher leads the students in practicing some new and old words: there, they, the, talk, tell. The teacher and students chant, write, and check the words. On-the-Back activity—word wall words with endings (suffixes): tells, talks, talking, telling, talked

Making Words: Make—he we in win new hen when inch chin chew chewing

Sort—related words: chew, chewing; rhymes

Transfer—flew then spin crew

A Sample Week for Working with Words
Second Grade

Monday

Word Wall: The teacher adds the following words: because, friends, school, they're, were. The teacher and students chant, write, and check the new words.

Making Words: Make—pet pest past last east least sheep sleep asleep please elephants

Sort—related words: sleep, asleep; rhymes

Transfer—feast steep creep blast

Tuesday

Word Wall: The teacher leads the students in practicing the new words: because, friends, school, they're, were. The teacher and students chant, write, and check the new words. On-the-Back activity—Be a Mind Reader with the new words

Reading/Writing Rhymes: The teacher uses the -ail/-ale patterns for this activity.

Wednesday

Word Wall: The teacher leads the students in practicing some new and old words: because, before, school, small, said. The teacher and students chant, write, and check the words. On-the-Back activity—words that rhyme with school and small: stool, fool, stall, squall, mall

Making Words: Make—am arm are Sam all mall sell smell small smear smaller

Sort—related words: small, smaller; sm, rhymes

Transfer—swell slam stall shell

Thursday

Word Wall: The teacher leads the students in practicing some new and old words: friends, from, were, when, will. The teacher and students chant, write, and check the words. On-the-Back activity—words that rhyme with when and will: then, hen, still, thrill, grill

Guess the Covered Word: The teacher uses a paragraph from the social studies book for this activity. She selects content area words to use as the covered words.

Friday

Word Wall: The teacher leads the students in practicing some new and old words: they're, there, their, want, write. The teacher and students chant, write, and check the words. On-the-Back activity—word wall words with endings (suffixes): wants, writer, writing, wanted, wanting

Using Words You Know: The teacher selects the following words, which she is sure her students know: went, ten, best, tell.

A Sample Week for Working with Words
Third Grade

Monday

Word Wall: The teacher adds the following words: anyone, discover, lovable, thought, you're. The teacher and students chant, write, and check the new words.

Using Words You Know: The teacher selects the following words, which he is sure his students know: thing, bang, song, hung.

Tuesday

Word Wall: The teacher leads the students in practicing the new words: anyone, discover, lovable, thought, you're. The teacher and students chant, write, and check the new words. On-the-Back activity—Be a Mind Reader with new words

Guess the Covered Word: The teacher uses a paragraph from the science textbook for this activity. He selects content area words to use as the covered words.

Wednesday

Word Wall: The teacher leads the students in practicing some new and old words: anyone, everybody, something, discover, recycle. The teacher and students chant, write, and check the words. On-the-Back activity—spell new words by combining parts of word wall words: recover, anything, anybody, everyone, someone

Making Words: Make—our use used sour sound round ground around garden danger dangerous

Sort—related words: use, used; round, around; danger, dangerous; rhymes

Transfer—mound pound flour bound

Thursday

Word Wall: The teacher leads the students in practicing some new and old words: you're, have, was, wouldn't, were. The teacher and students chant, write, and check the words. On-the-Back activity—spell new words by combining parts of word wall words: shouldn't, couldn't, wasn't, weren't, haven't

What Looks Right: The teacher uses -ail/-ale patterns for this activity.

Friday

Word Wall: The teacher leads the students in practicing some new and old words: lovable, exciting, friendly, prettier, prettiest. The teacher and students chant, write, and check the words. On-the-Back activity—spell new words by combining parts of word wall words: excitable, loving, lovely, lovelier, loveliest

Making Words: Make—not rot rip trip trot rope ripe ripen rotten protect protection

Sort—related words: ripe, ripen; rot, rotten, protect, protection; rhymes

Transfer—slip slot blip blot

CAUTION! THIS BLOCK UNDER CONSTRUCTION!

Common Roadblocks in Working with Words

It's not Four Blocks if you are not doing ALL four blocks every single day.
(Well, to be honest, almost every single day!)

It's NOT Four Blocks if you are putting topic-related words on the word wall.

Four-Blocks teachers do NOT clutter up the word wall with topic-related words. Word-wall space is reserved for high-frequency words and words with important patterns in them. In Four-Blocks classrooms, topic-related words are displayed on theme boards and charts.

It's NOT Four Blocks if you are taking words off of the word wall.

Four-Blocks teachers put important words on the word wall and leave them there all year. If words are important enough to go on the word wall, they need to stay there.

It's NOT Four Blocks if you simply have words on a wall.

Four-Blocks teachers don't just have a word wall; they DO the word wall. They include daily word-wall activities and are constantly reminding (nagging?) children to use the word wall when they write.

A Making Words lesson always has three parts: make, sort, and transfer.

Clever Four-Blocks teachers know a brisk pace is important for Making Words.

The focus of activities in the Working with Words Block is ALWAYS on transfer to reading and writing!

References

Professional References

Calkins, L. M. (1994) *The Art of Teaching Writing*. Portsmouth, NH: Heinemann.

Cunningham, P. M. (1999) *The Four-Blocks® Literacy Model: How and Why It Really Works*. (video) Greensboro, NC: Carson-Dellosa Publishing.

Cunningham, P. M. (1999) *Phonics They Use, 3rd edition*. New York: Addison-Wesley.

Cunningham, P. M. and Allington, R. L. (1994) *Classrooms That Work*. New York: Allyn and Bacon.

Cunningham, P. M. and Allington, R. L. (1999) *Classrooms That Work, 2nd edition*. New York: Allyn and Bacon.

Cunningham, P. M. and Hall, D. P. (1997) *Month-by-Month Phonics for First Grade*. Greensboro, NC: Carson-Dellosa Publishing.

Cunningham, P. M. and Hall, D. P. (1998) *Month-by-Month Phonics for Third Grade*. Greensboro, NC: Carson-Dellosa Publishing.

Cunningham, P. M. and Hall, D. P. (1998) *Month-by-Month for the Upper Grades*. Greensboro, NC: Carson-Dellosa Publishing

Cunningham, P. M.; Hall, D. P.; and Cunningham, J.W. (2000) *Guided Reading the Four-Blocks® Way*. Greensboro, NC: Carson-Dellosa Publishing.

Cunningham, P. M.; Hall, D. P.; and Cunningham, J.W. (2001) *Guided Reading* video series. Greensboro, NC: Carson-Dellosa Publishing.

Cunningham, P. M.; Hall, D. P.; and Defee, M. (1991) Non-ability grouped, multimethod instruction: A year in a first-grade classroom. *The Reading Teacher, 44*.

Cunningham, P. M.; Hall, D. P.; and Defee, M. (1998) Non-ability grouped, multimethod instruction: Eight years later. *The Reading Teacher, 51*.

Cunningham, P. M.; Hall, D. P.; and Gambrell, L. B. (2002) *Self-Selected Reading the Four-Blocks® Way*. Greensboro, NC: Carson-Dellosa Publishing.

Cunningham, P. M.; Hall, D. P.; and Sigmon, C. M. (1999, 2001) *The Teacher's Guide to Four Blocks®*. Greensboro, NC: Carson-Dellosa Publishing.

Graves, D. H. (1995) *A Fresh Look at Writing*. Portsmouth, NH: Heinemann.

Hall, D. P. and Cunningham, P. M. (1997) *Month-by-Month Reading and Writing for Kindergarten*. Greensboro, NC: Carson-Dellosa Publishing

Hall, D. P. and Cunningham, P. M. (1998) *Month-by-Month Phonics for Second Grade*. Greensboro, NC: Carson-Dellosa Publishing.

Hall, D. P.; Arens, A. B.; and Loman, K. L. (2002) *The Administrator's Guide to Building Blocks™*. Greensboro, NC: Carson-Dellosa Publishing.

Hall, D. P.; Cunningham, P. M.; Boger, D. (2002) *Writing Mini-Lessons for First Grade: The Four-Blocks® Model*. Greensboro, NC: Carson-Dellosa Publishing.

Hall, D. P.; Cunningham, P. M.; Smith, D. R. (2002) *Writing Mini-Lessons for Second Grade: The Four-Blocks® Model*. Greensboro, NC: Carson-Dellosa Publishing.

Hall, D. P.; Prevatte, C.; and Cunningham, P. M. (1995) Eliminating ability grouping and reducing failure in the primary grades. In Allington, R. L. and Walmsley, S. (Eds.) *No Quick Fix*. New York: Teachers College Press.

Routman, R. (1995) *Transitions, 2nd edition*. Portsmouth, NH: Heinemann.

Sigmon, C. M. and Ford, S. M. (2002) *Writing Mini-Lessons for Third Grade: The Four-Blocks® Model*. Greensboro, NC: Carson-Dellosa Publishing.

Veatch, J. (1959) *Individualizing Your Reading Program*. New York: Putnam.

References

Children's Works Cited

ABC I Like Me! by Nancy Carlson (Viking, 1997)

An Alphabet Book of Cats and Dogs by Sheila Moxley (Little, Brown and Co., 2001)

Animals in the Summer by Jane McCauley (National Geographic Society, 1988)

"The Big Chill" *Time for Kids* (Vol. 4, No. 17)

Billy and the Big New School by Catherine and Laurence Anholt (Albert Whitman Co., 1997)

Click, Clack, Moo: Cows That Type by Doreen Cronin (Simon and Schuster Publishers, 2000)

Donovan's Word Jar by Monalisa DeGross (HarperTrophy, 1994)

The Gingerbread Man by Alan Trussell-Cullen (Dominie Press, Inc., 1999)

Henry and Mudge: The First Book by Cynthia Rylant (Simon and Schuster, 1996)

I Like Jam by Stella Yang (Rigby, 2001)

I Wish that I Had Duck Feet by Theo. LeSieg (Random House, 1991)

If You Give a Mouse a Cookie by Laura Numeroff (HarperCollins, 1985)

Junie B., First Grader (at last!) by Barbara Park (Random House, 2001)

Kids in the Kitchen by Jill Eggleton (Rigby, 1999)

Little? I'm just the Right Size! by Mary E. Pearson (Steck-Vaughn Co., 2002)

Monkey-Monkey's Tricks by Patricia McKissack (Random House, Inc., 1988)

Mufaro's Beautiful Daughter by John Steptoe (Scholastic, Inc., 1987)

Oh, How I Wished I Could Read by John Gile (JGC/United Publishing Corps, 1995)

Over in the Meadow by Jane Cabrera (Holiday House Publishers, 1999)

Pigs by Gail Gibbons (Holiday House Publishers, 1999)

Polar the Titanic Bear by Daisy Cronin Stone Spedder (Little, Brown and Co., 1994)

The Scrubbing Machine by Joy Cowley (Wright Group, 1998)

See What I Can Do! by Mary E. Pearson (Steck-Vaughn Co., 2002)

Sunken Treasure by Gail Gibbons (HarperTrophy, 1990)

Third Grade Stinks! by Colleen O'Shaughnessy McKenna (Holiday House Publishers, 2001)

Titanic by Victoria Shaw (Scholastic, Inc., 1999)

The Titanic Lost . . . and Found by Judy Donnelly (Random House, 1987)

Tonight on the Titanic by Mary Pope Osborne (Random House, 1999)

The True Story of the Three Pigs by Jon Scieszka (Scholastic, Inc., 1989)

Understanding Electricity by Stephen M. Tomecek (National Geographic Society, 2002)

Weather in the City by George Wong (National Geographic Society, 2001)

Weather Today by Marvin Buckley (National Geographic Society, 2001)

"Welcome Baby Panda" *Time for Kids* (Vol. 5, No. 2)

When I Was Little by Jamie Lee Curtis (HarperCollins, 1993)

How Four Blocks Is a Comprehensive
Reading and Writing Instructional Framework and
Research that Supports Comprehensive Instruction

Most schools are currently working to implement research-based reading and writing instruction. In some cases, research is being used to support instruction that is very single-minded and narrowly focused. Instruction that is almost exclusively focused on phonics instruction, for example, will usually produce better reading achievement scores at the end of first grade. There is no evidence, however, that these initial gains can be sustained; in fact, there is evidence to the contrary. There is general agreement about the long-term goal of reading and writing instruction. Teachers want all children to go to middle school with the ability to think deeply about what they read and to express themselves clearly and persuasively through their writing. Teachers want avid and enthusiastic readers and writers who continue to grow in these avenues of communication and learning throughout their lives. Producing avid, enthusiastic, thoughtful, critical readers and writers requires that teachers provide students with comprehensive instruction that focuses on and develops all the essential strategies and attributes. What are the components of a comprehensive reading and writing curriculum? There is a strong research base for the inclusion of six components in a comprehensive reading and writing curriculum:

- word identification instruction, including phonemic awareness, phonics and fluency
- comprehension instruction
- daily time devoted to teacher read-aloud
- daily time devoted to independent reading
- vocabulary instruction as part of reading instruction, as well as science and social studies instruction
- instruction and time for writing—both for its own sake and as another avenue through which children can become better readers.

Four Blocks is a framework for reading and writing that includes all of the components of a comprehensive instructional program. Teacher read-aloud and independent reading are included during the Self-Selected Reading Block. Comprehension instruction is included during Guided Reading. Phonics, including phonemic awareness, is taught during Working with Words. Fluency is developed as children learn to read and spell high-frequency words during the Word Wall activity and when teachers preform repeated readings during Guided Reading. Writing instruction is included during the Writing Block. Meaning vocabulary is taught during Guided Reading, especially when teachers include science and social studies material during Guided Reading. Meaning vocabulary is also developed during Self-Selected Reading as children listen to what the teacher reads aloud and engage in regular independent reading. Following is a summary of the research that supports the inclusion of these components in a comprehensive reading and writing instructional program.

Word Identification Instruction

Systematic instruction in how to identify words is essential for most children to become good and avid readers. The current phonics debate is more about what should be included in word identification instruction and what form that instruction should take than about whether to include it in the curriculum. There is general support from research for systematic phonics and phonemic awareness instruction, as well as attention to oral reading fluency.

Phonics Instruction

There have been few instructional studies comparing different types of phonics instruction, and those studies that have been done have often compared systematic phonics instruction with "hit-or-miss" phonics instruction. From these studies, one can conclude that any kind of well-organized and efficient phonics instruction is generally better than little or no phonics instruction that leaves learning phonics to chance. Stahl, Duffy-Hester, and Stahl (1998) reviewed the research on phonics instruction and concluded that there are several types of good phonics instruction and there is no research base to support the superiority of any one particular type. The National Reading Panel (NRP) (2000a; 2000b) reviewed the experimental research on teaching phonics and determined that explicit and systematic phonics is superior to nonsystematic or no phonics, but that there is no significant difference in effectiveness among the kinds of systematic phonics instruction. They also found no significant difference in effectiveness among tutoring, small-group, or whole-class phonics instruction.

Put Reading First (Armbruster, Lehr, and Osborn, 2001) summarizes the findings of the NRP report and makes instructional recommendations based on these findings. In *Put Reading First*, a useful definition of systematic phonics is included:

> A program of systematic phonics instruction clearly identifies a carefully selected and useful set of letter-sound relationships and then organizes the introduction of these relationships into a logical instructional sequence. The instructional sequence may include the relationships between the sounds associated with single letters (for example, the sound /m/ with the letter **m**) as well as with larger units of written language (for example, letter combinations such as **th** or **ing** or spelling patterns such as **ea** or **ie**). Furthermore, a systematic program of instruction provides children with ample opportunities to practice the relationships they are learning. (page 16)

Put Reading First also offers the following guidelines for effective phonics instruction:

- teachers explicitly and systematically instruct students in how to relate letters and sounds, how to break spoken words into sounds, and how to blend sounds to form words;

- students understand why they are learning the relationships between letters and sounds;

- students apply their knowledge of phonics as they read words, sentences and text;

- students apply what they learn about sounds and letters to their own writing;

- can be adapted to the needs of individual students, based on assessment;

- includes alphabetic knowledge, phonemic awareness, vocabulary development, and the reading of text as well as systematic phonics instruction. (page 16)

Another issue related to how phonics instruction can be most effectively taught relates to when and for how long phonics instruction should take place. *Put Reading First* recommends that phonics instruction be completed by the end of first or second grade and summarizes the research on phonics instruction with older children:

> Systematic phonics instruction by itself may not be enough to significantly improve the overall reading and spelling performance of reading beyond first grade. The effects of phonics instruction

---

on students in second through sixth grades are limited to improving their word reading and oral text reading skills. The effects do not extend to spelling and reading comprehension. For these students, it is important to emphasize reading fluency and comprehension. In addition, these students also require explicit spelling instruction to improve their spelling. (page 18)

Because systematic phonics instruction is better than nonsystematic or no phonics instruction, but does not result in improved spelling or reading comprehension past first grade, a comprehensive program will include instructional attention to phonics, oral reading fluency, and comprehension from the beginning. The recommendation to complete all phonics instruction by the end of second grade, however, seems shortsighted when one considers the changing nature of new words encountered in the text students read beginning in third grade. In 1984, Nagy and Anderson published a landmark study in which they analyzed a sample of 7,260 words found in books commonly read by students in grades three through nine. They found that most of these words were polysyllabic words and that many of these big words were related semantically through their morphology. Some of these relationships are easily noticed. The words hunter, redness, foglights, and stringy are clearly related to the words hunt, red, fog, and string. Other more complex word relationships exist between words such as planet; planetarium, vicious; vice, and apart; apartment. Nagy and Anderson hypothesized that if children knew or learned how to interpret morphological relationships, they would know six or seven words for every basic word known.

Phonics can be defined simply as understanding about the relationships between letters and sounds. Nagy and Anderson's 1984 research shows a large percentage of the new words encountered beginning in third grade are polysyllabic words related through their morphology-base words, prefixes and suffixes. If phonics instruction is completed by the end of first or second grade, where will readers learn the morphemic relationships necessary to decode the polysyllabic words encountered in text beginning in third grade? Teaching morphemic letter-sound relationships to decode big words has not been widely investigated and thus does not have an adequate research base to support it. Logic, however, suggests that because phonics instruction with the vowel/consonant patterns that comprise most short words is effective in helping children read them, instruction with the morphemic patterns that make up most polysyllabic words would also be helpful. This instruction might be included as part of the spelling program or as part of meaning vocabulary development, but it should be integrated with what students already know about decoding. What is important here is that teachers recognize that most of the new words that readers have to decode beginning in third grade are polysyllabic, and they cannot be decoded based on the simple letter patterns found in one-syllable words. A comprehensive reading and writing curriculum should include how morphemes help students decode, spell, and access or build meaning for big words. Surely, it would help to include the features of systematic phonics instruction that emphasize careful teaching and many opportunities to apply what is taught.

A Word of Caution about Phonics

While there is research support for systematic phonics instruction from the beginning of reading instruction, studies also suggest that this method will not work for all children. It can be overemphasized, and newer spelling-based phonics approaches may work better for below-average readers.

Wise and Olson (1995) discovered that reading-disabled children who learned the most from synthetic phonics instruction did not transfer this improvement to real-word reading, neither immediately nor even after one or two years. Torgesen, Wagner, and Rashotte (1997) found a similar result with their participants who had serious reading disabilities.

Juel, Biancarosa, Coker, and Deffes (2002) found that an overemphasis on letter-sound instruction in first grade negatively affected the development of oral meaning vocabulary knowledge for some children.

Newer approaches to teaching phonics often use guided and independent spelling activities to teach letter-sound relationships and their application (P. Cunningham, 2000; Stahl, Duffy-Hester and Stahl, 1998). A number of studies support integrating phonics and spelling instruction with young children (for example, Cataldo and Ellis, 1988; Ehri and Wilce, 1987; Ellis and Cataldo, 1990). For instance, Clarke (1988) found that first-grade programs that included invented spelling produced better decoders than first-grade programs that included only traditional spelling. Uhry and Shepherd (1993) also found that including spelling as part of the word instruction first graders receive improved their decoding. More recently, Davis (2000) found that spelling-based decoding instruction was as effective as reading-based decoding instruction for all of her students, but more effective for the children with poor phonological awareness.

Juel and Minden-Cupp (2000) noted that, of the teachers they observed, the most effective teachers of children who entered first grade with few literacy skills combined systematic letter-sound instruction with onset-rime compare-contrast activities instruction, and emphasized application to reading and writing.

Phonemic Awareness Instruction

In addition to systematic phonics instruction, there is a great deal of research support for phonemic awareness instruction (National Reading Panel, 2000b). Phonemic awareness is the realization that spoken words are made up of sounds. These sounds (phonemes) are not separate and distinct. In fact, their existence is quite abstract (Shankweiler, 1999). Phonemic awareness has many levels and includes the ability to decide whether spoken words rhyme, to know what spoken word you would have if you removed a sound, to segment words into sounds, and to blend separate sounds into words. Phonemic awareness seems to develop gradually for most children through much exposure to nursery rhymes and books that promote word play (Yopp and Yopp, 2000).

Phonemic awareness is one of the best predictors of success in learning to read (Bryant, Bradley, Maclean, and Crossland, 1989; National Reading Panel, 2000b). Perhaps because it is such a good predictor of beginning reading, some schools and teachers have overemphasized phonemic awareness. Large amounts of time given to phonemic awareness activities each day means neglecting other activities that are important to literacy, such as the development of oral language and meaning vocabulary, listening comprehension, and print concepts. In fact, *Put Reading First* makes the specific recommendation that: "Over the school year, your entire phonemic awareness program should take no more than 20 hours." (page 9) Allocating 30-40 minutes per week (not the 30-40 minutes per day observed in some classrooms) will ensure that phonemic awareness is emphasized but not overemphasized.

A Word of Caution about Phonemic Awareness

Torgesen and Davis (1996) concluded that even extensive phonemic awareness training does not succeed with children who are severely disabled in phonological processes. Catts, Fey, Zhang, and Tomblin (1999) found that the children who most lacked phonemic awareness often benefited least from phonemic awareness instruction, especially if their oral vocabularies were also weak.

Byrne and Fielding-Barnsley (1995) reported that even successful phonemic awareness instruction was much more likely to transfer to later decoding ability than to later word recognition and oral reading fluency abilities. If teachers consider phonemic awareness instruction to be adequate preparation for being able to learn to read, they may ignore the other kinds of preparation that make it easier to learn to read.

Ellis and Cataldo (1990), the National Reading Panel (2000b), and Davis (2000) all found that working with letters aided phonemic awareness instruction. Yet working with letters makes phonemic awareness instruction synonymous with phonics instruction (Yopp and Yopp, 2000). It is important not to start such instruction too early.

Oral Reading Fluency Instruction

All of this attention to research supporting systematic phonics instruction and up to 20 hours of phonemic awareness instruction annually might lead one to conclude that reading is carried out by decoding each word as that word is encountered. In fact, it is only the most struggling readers who decode most words as they read. Good readers recognize most words automatically—that is, quickly, with little or no effort, as a unit (A. Cunningham, Perry, and Stanovich, 2001; Gustafson, 2001; Lee, Honig, and Lee, 2002; Logan, 1997).

Readers who automatically recognize most words in a text and can simultaneously do the other things that reading requires (J. Cunningham, 1993) are reading that text with fluency. Fluency is the ability to read most words in context quickly, accurately, automatically, and with appropriate expression. Fluency is critical to reading comprehension because of the attention factor. The human brain can attend to a limited number of things at a time. If most of the attention is focused on decoding the words, there is little attention left for the comprehension part of reading—putting the words together and thinking about what they mean. The NRP Summary explains this relationship between reading comprehension and fluency thusly: "If text is read in a laborious and inefficient manner, it will be difficult for the child to remember what has been read and to relate the ideas expressed in the text to his or her background knowledge." (page 11)

Fluency is not something a reader has or does not have. In fact, fluency is directly related to the complexity of the text being read. For example, a text with many words that has been read accurately many times before will prompt the reader to recognize those familiar words immediately and automatically. Some attention can then be focused on the meaning of what is being read. However, a text with many words that have never been encountered in print before will require the reader to stop and decode these words in some way—using the letter-sound and morphemic patterns knowledge to turn the printed letters into sounds and words. In order to comprehend what has been decoded, the reader may have to reread the text once or even twice so that attention is freed from decoding and available for comprehending.

Research supports two different approaches to helping students become more fluent oral readers. First, teachers should read aloud to children and have the children reread texts orally to improve their accuracy, rate, and expression. Second, teachers should teach students to spell the most common words in books and other reading materials.

Teacher Read-Aloud and Repeated Oral Readings

Many opportunities for successful reading are essential for the development of fluency. "Fluency develops as a result of many opportunities to practice reading with a high degree of success. Therefore, your students should practice orally rereading text that is reasonably easy for them—that is, text containing mostly words that they know or can decode easily." (*Put Reading First*, page 27)

In English, approximately 300 words make up 85% of the running words in almost all the text that is read (Samuels, 2002). Recognizing these high-frequency words accurately and automatically promotes fluent reading. While practice with these high-frequency words in isolation can help children learn these words, that word learning will not necessarily transfer to reading words in text unless extensive practice in reading interesting and meaningful text is provided (J. Cunningham, Koppenhaver, Erickson, and Spadorcia, in press).

Put Reading First recommends two activities for increasing reading fluency: reading aloud to children and engaging children in repeated readings of instructional-level text. The many reasons why a comprehensive literacy program includes daily teacher read-aloud will be summarized later, in the reading-aloud-to-children section of this review. As it relates specifically to fluency, however, *Put Reading First* recommends: "By listening to good models of fluent reading, students learn how a reader's voice can help written text make sense. Read aloud daily to your students. By reading effortlessly and with expression, you are modeling for your students how a fluent reader sounds during reading." (page 26)

Even more important than the teacher modeling good oral reading is having children read instructional-level texts more than once to improve how fluently they read the texts. To accomplish repeated readings without boredom setting in, *Put Reading First* recommends the use of plays and poetry using such formats as adult-then-student reading (echo reading), choral reading, tape-assisted reading, partner reading, and readers' theater. When meaning is emphasized during repeated readings, children can also be taught how to read with better expression (Erekson, 2001).

Spelling-based Word Recognition Instruction

Early on, word identification and spelling seem to be strictly separate processes (Bryant and Bradley, 1980). By the end of first grade, however, they have become highly related to each other (Bryant and Bradley, 1980; Gough, Juel, and Griffith, 1992). Correlations between the two are quite high (Ehri, 1997; Zutell, 1992), in spite of dampening from the well-known fact that most children can identify words they are unable to spell (Bosman and Van Orden, 1997; Perfetti, 1997). The high relationship appears to derive from the opposite condition that children beyond the beginning can almost always pronounce a word accurately that they can spell correctly (Hall, 1991).

These studies make it very plausible that teaching students to spell words is one way to teach the students to recognize those words. A few other studies have investigated this possibility more directly. For example, Uhry and Shepherd (1993) found that including spelling as part of the word instruction first graders receive improved their word recognition. Logan (1997) presents evidence that automatic word recognition is not a general skill or ability, but how well each word is known. He further argues that how well each word is known is in part a function of how much it has been studied. Learning to spell words is one way of carefully studying them. It seems prudent to begin no later than spring of first grade to teach children to correctly spell the 300 most common words in printed English as an aid to their automatic word recognition for those words and hence children's oral reading fluency.

A Word of Caution about Oral Reading Fluency

Good oral reading does not guarantee comprehension. This can be easily proven by reading articles aloud from academic journals in fields one knows little about. Moreover, an overemphasis on oral reading fluency may give some students the impression that silent reading comprehension is unimportant. These commonsense understandings draw support from research showing that it is poor readers rather than good readers who have received a greater relative and absolute amount of oral reading instruction (Allington, 1983, 1984).

Summary of Research on the Word Identification Component

The research on word identification instruction is quite clear, and there is a general consensus on a number of key issues. Children profit from systematic phonics instruction, but there is no one best systematic method. Children need many opportunities to apply what they are learning in phonics to their own reading and writing. Phonemic awareness is important to success in reading and can be accomplished with a maximum of 20 hours of instruction annually. Fluency, the ability to read words in text quickly, accurately and with expression, is essential for comprehension. Oral reading fluency is best developed through the modeling of teacher read-alouds and reading and rereading of easy materials and is indirectly facilitated by teaching students to spell the most commonly printed words.

Reading Comprehension Instruction

Comprehension—thinking about and responding to what you are reading—is "what it's all about!" Comprehension is the reason for and prime motivator for engaging in reading. What comprehension is, how comprehension occurs, and how to teach comprehension have driven hundreds of research studies in the last 30 years. Reading comprehension, and how to teach it, is probably the area of literacy about which there is the most knowledge and the most consensus. It is also probably the area that gets the least attention in the classroom.

In 1978, Delores Durkin published a landmark study demonstrating that there was little, if any, reading comprehension instruction happening in most classrooms and that the small amount that did occur was "mentioning" rather than teaching. Having children answer comprehension questions to assess their reading comprehension was the main activity most often seen. This finding shocked the reading community and probably propelled much of the reading comprehension research that has occurred since. Unfortunately, more recent research (Beck, McKeown and Gromoll, 1989; Pressley and Wharton-McDonald, 1998) indicates that reading comprehension instruction is still a rare commodity in most elementary classrooms.

One important type of reading comprehension research has focused on the characteristics of good comprehenders. Duke and Pearson (2002) summarize what good readers do. Good readers:

- are active and have clear goals in mind.

- preview text before reading, make predictions, and read selectively to meet their goals.

- construct, revise, and question the meanings they are making as they read.

- try to determine the meanings of unfamiliar words and concepts.

- draw from, compare, and integrate their prior knowledge with what they are reading.

- monitor their understanding and make adjustments as needed.

- think about the authors of the text and evaluate the text's quality and value.

- read different kinds of text differently, paying attention to characters and settings when reading narratives, constructing and revising summaries in their minds when reading expository text.

Knowing that good readers have and use a variety of comprehension strategies, many researchers have investigated the effects of teaching students these strategies. *Put Reading First* defines comprehension strategies as "conscious plans—sets of steps that good readers use to make sense of text." (page 49) According to the NRP report, there is substantial evidence to support the teaching of the following six comprehension strategies:

(1.) monitoring comprehension.

(2.) using graphic and semantic organizers.

(3.) answering questions.

(4.) generating questions.

(5.) recognizing story structure.

(6.) summarizing.

According to the NRP report, there is also some research support for two other strategies:

(7.) using prior knowledge.

(8.) using mental imagery.

Duke and Pearson (2002), in their review of research, identify six research-based strategies:

(1.) prediction/activation of prior knowledge.

(2.) think-alouds (which includes monitoring comprehension).

(3.) using text structure.

(4.) using/constructing visual representations (including graphic organizers and imagery).

(5.) summarization.

(6.) answering questions/questioning.

A comparison of Duke and Pearson's list with the NRP list shows a remarkable amount of agreement on which strategies, if taught, produce measurable gains in reading comprehension.

The final question to be considered is how these comprehension strategies can be most effectively taught. Again, there is a great deal of consensus. Both the NRP and the Duke and Pearson reviews suggest that explicit teaching, including an explanation of what and how the strategy should be used, teacher modeling and thinking aloud about the strategy, guided practice with the strategy, and support for students applying the strategy independently are the steps needed to effectively teach any comprehension strategy. Both support the use of cooperative learning groups working together to apply the strategies to text. Both suggest that because comprehension is not achieved by using only one of the strategies, lessons which combine comprehension strategies are most effective. For example, reciprocal teaching (Palinscar and Brown, 1984), a cooperative learning format in which students work together to use the strategies of questioning, summarizing, clarifying, and predicting, is one way to organize instruction that incorporates both cooperative learning and combining strategies.

Earlier reviews of research on teaching reading comprehension found that a number of specific lesson frames can improve reading comprehension ability (Pearson and Fielding, 1991; Tierney and J. Cunningham, 1984). Most of these lesson frames have in common that they include guidance throughout and links among before-, during-, and after-reading activities. They each teach one or more strategies that appear in one of the lists (see page 66) with explicitness, application, or both.

Duke and Pearson also found that it is better to teach a variety of comprehension strategies rather than relying on one or a few. For example, they cite a research base for SAIL (Students Achieving Independent Learning). Comprehension strategies taught in SAIL (Pressley, et al, 1994) include predicting, visualizing, questioning, clarifying, making associations between text and reader's experience, and summarizing. In SAIL, students observe teacher think-alouds and then practice applying these strategies to a variety of texts.

A Word of Caution about Reading Comprehension

Reading comprehension, correctly and broadly understood, probably cannot be overemphasized. However, comprehension lessons and comprehension outcomes can become such a focus of teaching that teachers forget that a major goal of literacy instruction is for reading to become intrinsically motivating to students. Teachers want students to learn to enjoy reading for its own sake, something they can and will do outside of school with no prospect of external notice or reward. Teacher read-aloud and independent silent reading are among the best ways to build intrinsic motivation to read. Reading comprehension instruction, as essential as it is, must not be seen as a substitute for teacher read-aloud and independent silent reading, or their long-term benefits for all children may be decreased or lost.

Summary of Research on the Reading Comprehension Component

A great deal is known about how good readers comprehend, what the comprehension strategies are, and how to teach them. Our job now is to implement a well-planned program of reading comprehension instruction in every elementary classroom. Children need to focus on meaning and learn strategies for making meaning from the very beginning. *Put Reading First* summarizes the important role of reading comprehension instruction at all grade levels.

> Teachers should emphasize text comprehension from the beginning, rather than waiting until students have mastered "the basics" of reading. Instruction at all grade levels can benefit from showing students how reading is a process of making sense out of text, or constructing meaning. Beginning readers, as well as more advanced readers, must understand that the ultimate goal of reading is comprehension. (page 55)

Independent Silent Reading

Most educators and many research studies support the importance of the amount of reading students do. Allington (1977) and Biemiller (1977) concluded that students who are the poorest readers spend the least amount of time actually reading. Nagy and Anderson (1984) showed that good readers often read 10 times as many words as poor readers during the school day. Data collected from the 1996 National Assessment of Educational Progress (NAEP) testing indicated that 13-year-olds who reported more independent reading demonstrated better reading comprehension of both narrative and expository text than 17-year-olds who reported less independent reading (Campbell, Voelkl, and Donahue, 1997). In other words, middle school students who read more were better readers than high school students who had completed four more years of schooling! Stanovich (1986) labeled the tendency of poor readers to remain poor readers as "The Matthew Effect" and attributed the increasing gap between good readers and poor readers in part to the difference in time spent reading.

Wide reading is highly correlated with meaning vocabulary, which, in turn, is highly correlated with reading comprehension. Students who read more encounter the same words more frequently, and repeated exposures to the same words have been shown to lead to improvements in fluency (Topping and Paul, 1999). A. Cunningham and Stanovich (1998) found that struggling readers with limited reading and comprehension skills increased vocabulary and comprehension skills when time spent reading was increased.

Wide reading is also associated with the development of automatic word recognition (Stanovich and West, 1989). Share (1995; 1999) has reviewed the research evidence for his contention that self-teaching of word recognition occurs while a reader is decoding words during independent reading. Good decoders teach themselves to recognize many words as they read for enjoyment.

> The practice of independent silent reading has come under scrutiny recently because of the National Reading Panel conclusion that independent silent reading did not support fluency. Samuels (2002), who was a member of the National Reading Panel, points out that the National Reading Panel report did not recommend independent silent reading as a way to improve fluency because of the lack of support through experimental studies. ". . . the NRP decided it would not accept correlational studies, of which there are a substantial number showing a positive relationship between various measures of reading achievement and time spent reading." (page 174)

One of the many studies ignored by the NRP, because it used correlational data and was not an experiment, was conducted by Cipielewski and Stanovich (1992). In this study, Cipielewski and Stanovich attempted to sort out the "chicken or egg" question that clouds much of the correlational research showing that good readers read more. Are children good readers because they read more, or do children read more because they are good readers?

To help them decide, Cipielewski and Stanovich compared reading comprehension scores at the end of third and fifth grade and included a measure of the amount of reading which they called print exposure. To estimate print exposure, they used a Title Recognition Test (TRT) and an Author Recognition Test (ART). Students were asked to select titles and authors which were real books and real authors from a list that included some real titles and authors and some foils. Results of the hierarchal regression analysis indicated that scores on both the TRT and the ART explained significant additional variance after third grade reading scores were partialed out.

The authors of this study point out that this was a very conservative test of the effect of reading on comprehension because some effect for print exposure would already have been present in the third grade scores.

> By entering third-grade reading comprehension ability into the regression equation prior to the TRT and ART we do not mean to imply that we believe that print exposure has no influence on comprehension . . . prior to the third grade . . . . We nevertheless allowed third-grade comprehension to appropriate variance that rightly belongs to print exposure, in order to deliberately bias the analyses against the last variable . . . . Print exposure appears to be both a consequence of developed reading ability and a contributor to further growth in that ability. (page 85)

Another kind of information that was ignored by the NRP because it was not experimental research comes from surveys. In 1975, Sterl Artley asked college students what they remembered teachers doing that prompted their interest and competence in reading. The vast majority of the respondents gave teacher read-aloud and time for independent reading as major factors in their reading development. Recently, Ivey and Broaddus (2001) surveyed

1,765 sixth graders to determine what motivates them to read. The responses of this large group of diverse preteens indicated that their motivation for reading came from having time for independent reading in books of their own choosing and from teachers reading aloud to them.

Experiments, by their very nature, are short-term interventions. The studies reviewed by the NRP that did not find reading comprehension gains when children were given time for independent reading were, for the most part, carried out across weeks. The study most prominently cited (Carver and Leibert, 1995) spanned a six-week summer program in which the children read on average for a total of 24 hours. The lack of comprehension gained after 24 hours of independent reading should not be a surprise. Comprehension is a complex act in which motivation, background knowledge, vocabulary, strategy use, interest, and type of text all play a role. There are also problems in measuring comprehension and comprehension gains.

A Word of Caution about Independent Silent Reading

While independent silent reading is definitely associated with long-term growth in reading ability, it should not be seen as a substitute for word identification or comprehension instruction. At times in the past, the recognized advantages of independent silent reading have led some to think of it as a sufficient activity—"you learn to read by reading." Because most children need more direct word identification and reading comprehension instruction to learn how to read well, independent silent reading should be seen as providing complementary applications of those kinds of instruction, rather than as replacements for them.

Summary of Research on the Independent Silent Reading Component

The vast body of research which looks at reading achievement and motivation in a long-term way supports the practice of providing time and motivation for independent silent reading. Samuels (2002) recommends independent silent reading but emphasizes that if independent silent reading will increase the amount of reading done by poor readers, teachers should help students with book selection so that they don't choose books that are too hard and then stop reading. He also stresses that students should read books they find enjoyable so that they are motivated to read further. Samuels concludes that, "Increasing the amount of reading students do is important, because as words are encountered repeatedly there are a number of beneficial outcomes, such as improvements in word recognition, speed, ease of reading, and comprehension." (page 174)

Teacher Read-Aloud

It is hard to overstate the importance of reading aloud to children as a regular and scheduled part of daily instruction in every elementary classroom. Research has been cited in previous sections of this review which demonstrates that reading aloud to children is an important factor in developing oral reading fluency and motivation to read. Reading to children is also an important avenue for incidental meaning vocabulary learning.

Elley (1989) found that 7- and 8-year-old children in New Zealand learned new word meanings incidentally from being read to and remembered those word meanings months later. He also found that below-average children learned about as many word meanings from teacher read-aloud as did above-average children.

Similarly, Stahl, Richek, and Vandevier (1991) found that sixth graders in a U.S. urban school acquired a significant number of new word meanings from being read to. Again, there was no difference between children with low versus high previous word meaning knowledge, and even the lowest children learned word meanings when they were read a book above grade level.

Put Reading First supports this aspect of teacher read-aloud and also advocates conversations with children about books they have heard read aloud:

> Children learn word meanings from listening to adults read to them. Reading aloud is particularly helpful when the reader pauses during reading to define an unfamiliar word and, after reading, engages the child in a conversation about a book. Conversations about books help children to

learn new words and concepts and to relate them to their prior knowledge and experience. (page 35)

Morrow and Gambrell (2000) summarized the research on reading-aloud to children and concluded that "children in the experimental classrooms who were read to daily over long periods of time scored significantly better on measures of vocabulary, comprehension and decoding ability than children in the control groups who were not read to by an adult." (page 568)

Reading aloud to children at home before they start school has been shown to be correlated with success in learning to read. According to Morrow and Gambrell (2000), children who had been read to frequently before coming to school had increased syntactic and vocabulary development, increased desire and motivation to learn to read, and more developed concepts of print.

In 1985, the National Institute of Education's *Becoming a Nation of Readers* stated that "the single most important activity for building the knowledge required for eventual success in reading is reading aloud to children." (Anderson, Hiebert, Scott, and Wilkinson, 1985, page 23)

According to Chasen and Gambrell (1992), the practice of daily read-alouds in K-3 classrooms increased greatly since the 1970s. Their survey found that 75% of teachers reported reading aloud on a daily basis in 1990 as opposed to only 45% of the teachers in 1980. In 1994, Lehman, Freeman, and Allen stated that 85% of elementary teachers reported reading aloud to their students at least once a day.

Currently, educators are in an era of "immediate accountability." Teachers are asked to demonstrate quarterly, weekly, and daily how the activities in their classrooms contribute to the reading achievement of the children they teach. It is not possible to measure the effects of teacher read-aloud on a daily, weekly, or even quarterly basis. Teacher read-aloud is clearly associated with increased vocabulary, comprehension, fluency and motivation to read. Teachers must be encouraged to continue their practice of reading aloud to students and have faith that in the long-term, this well-established practice will contribute to the development of avid and able readers.

A Word of Caution about Teacher Read-Aloud

Reading aloud to children has many advantages, but it should never be used as a substitute for instruction or independent silent reading. In the past, some schools and teachers have chosen not to provide children with materials they can read at an appropriate level of difficulty, but have chosen instead to read aloud the books they had. For the reasons given in this review, teacher read-aloud has much value, but it cannot replace the need for students to learn to comprehend the language of texts while simultaneously identifying the words and processing the print beyond what word identification requires (J. Cunningham, Koppenhaver, Erickson, and Spadorcia, in press). Teacher read-aloud is an essential component of a comprehensive reading and writing program, but it does not, by itself, teach either reading or writing.

Summary of Research on the Teacher Read-Aloud Component

Research supports that teacher read-aloud helps children acquire oral reading fluency, motivation to read, and meaning vocabulary knowledge. Recent studies have also shown that teacher read-aloud is now a widely-accepted component of a complete reading program.

Meaning Vocabulary Development

As teachers try to close the achievement gap and make high levels of literacy attainable for all children, they must pay renewed attention to the issue of meaning vocabulary. In 1977, Becker identified lack of vocabulary as a crucial factor underlying the failure of many disadvantaged students. In 1995, Hart and Risley described a relationship between growing up in poverty and restricted vocabulary. Biemiller and Slonim (2001) cite evidence that lack of vocabulary is a key component underlying school failure for disadvantaged students. More and more of the children we teach in our public schools are English language learners. The limited English vocabularies of many of these children is sure to impede their reading and writing of English text.

The size of the average child's meaning vocabulary (sometimes called oral vocabulary) is difficult to estimate because of the issue of what it means to know a word, but vocabulary growth in the preschool and elementary school years occurs daily and amazes everyone who observes it. Estimates are that elementary school children acquire some level of meaning for an average of seven new words per day (Nagy and Herman, 1987). The staggering number of words for which children have some level of meaning cannot be attributed to direct teaching of those words. Few parents engage in direct teaching of word meanings with their preschool children, and teachers could not possibly teach enough words directly to account for the size of the average elementary school child's vocabulary. Researchers now agree that most meaning vocabulary is learned indirectly. There is also a research base to support the direct teaching of vocabulary and word learning strategies (Baumann, Kame'enui, and Ash, 2003; Graves and Watts-Taffe, 2002; NRP, 2000b; Stahl and Fairbanks, 1986). Research on how meaning vocabulary is learned and how to effectively teach it leads to the inescapable conclusion that elementary classroom instruction should provide many opportunities for indirect learning of vocabulary and also include direct teaching of both vocabulary and vocabulary learning strategies.

Providing Opportunities for Indirect Learning of Vocabulary

How can teachers promote indirect learning of vocabulary? "Students learn vocabulary indirectly when they hear and see words used in many different contexts—for example, through conversations with adults, through being read to and through reading extensively on their own." (*Put Reading First*, page 35)

Earlier in this review, research was cited to support two of the major indirect routes for helping students acquire meaning vocabulary knowledge—teacher read-aloud and independent silent reading. Two other indirect routes also deserve mention here: conversations (Armbruster, Lehr and Osborn, 2001) and promoting word consciousness (Graves and Watts-Taffe, 2002). There are many opportunities for conversations throughout the classroom day. Teachers should seize these opportunities and promote teacher-student talk and student-student talk about current events, the weather, what students are reading, what students are writing, science and social studies topics, art, music, recess, classroom issues and problems, and other daily events. If someone were observing these "spontaneous" conversations, it might not be obvious that something academic is happening, but a great deal of vocabulary learning occurs indirectly, and conversations at home and at school are one source for this indirect learning.

A final way of promoting indirect learning of vocabulary is for teachers to strive to develop a sense of "word wonder" in their students. In spite of the difficulty of ever finding a definitive research-based answer to the relationship between word wonder and vocabulary development, there is general agreement among vocabulary researchers that "word consciousness" plays an important role in vocabulary learning. Graves and Watts-Taffe (2002) explain why word consciousness matters:

> Students who are word conscious are aware of the words around them—those they read and hear and those they write and speak. This awareness involves an appreciation of the power of words, an understanding of why certain words are used instead of others, a sense of the words that could be used in place of those selected by a writer or speaker, and cognizance of first encounters with new words. It involves an interest in learning and using new words and becoming more skillful and precise in word usage. . . . With tens of thousands of words to learn and with most of this word learning taking place incidentally as learners are reading and listening, the positive affective and cognitive disposition toward words that we are labeling "word consciousness" is crucial to learners' success in expanding the breadth and depth of their word knowledge over the course of their lifetimes. (pages 144-145)

Put Reading First also recommends developing word consciousness and some ways to create students who "enjoy words and are eager to learn new words . . . . Call their attention to the way authors choose words to convey particular meanings. Encourage students to play with words by engaging in word play, such as puns or palindromes. Help them research a word's origin or history. You can also encourage them to search for examples of a word's usage in their everyday lives." (page 44)

Direct Teaching of Vocabulary and Word Learning Strategies

Research supports the direct teaching of some words and the teaching of vocabulary learning strategies (Baumann, Kame'enui, and Ash, 2003; Blachowicz and Fisher, 2000; NRP, 2000b; Graves and Watts-Taffe, 2002). All sources indicate that the number of words directly taught must be kept to a minimum because the words need to be thoroughly taught and students need to meet them in a number of different contexts across some span of time. *Put Reading First* recommends limiting the new vocabulary words to 8-10 per week and teaching these words thoroughly. Because of the need to limit the number of words, teachers must carefully choose the words to be taught, giving preference to those words which are important, useful, and apt to occur many different times and in different contexts. "Children learn words best when they are provided with instruction over an extended period of time and when that instruction has them work actively with the words. The more students use new words and the more they use them in different contexts, the more likely they are to learn the words." (*Put Reading First*, page 36)

The need for children to actively encounter the words in different contexts over an extended period of time leads the NRP to recommend choosing many of the words for direct teaching from content area subjects.

> Vocabulary words should be words that the learner will find useful in many contexts. To that end, a large portion of vocabulary items should be derived from content learning materials. This would serve at least two functions: first, it would assist the learner in dealing with the specific reading matter in content area materials; second, it would provide the learner with vocabulary that would be encountered sufficiently often to make the learning effort worthwhile. (NRP, 2000b, page 4-25f)

In addition to the direct teaching of a limited number of useful, frequently-occurring words, there is support in the research for teaching children word learning strategies. These word-learning strategies fall into three major categories: (1) learning to use context clues to determine word meanings; (2) learning to use dictionaries and other word resources; and (3) learning to use morphemic information-base words, prefixes and suffixes to figure out meanings for words. If, while teaching children from third grade and above to use this morphemic information for meaning, teachers would also emphasize how these morphemic parts are the keys to pronouncing polysyllabic words, the previously expressed concerns about completing all phonics instruction by the end of second grade would be greatly alleviated.

A Word of Caution about Meaning Vocabulary

There is no evidence in the research that giving students a vocabulary list and having them learn a definition which they then "parrot back" on a test will result in long-term vocabulary growth or increase reading comprehension. Additionally, there is no evidence to support having students study words from a commercially produced vocabulary program which provides a weekly list of words unrelated to the curriculum and not apt to be seen or heard in any context other than in the program itself. Vocabulary can and should be taught, but the way in which it is taught and the emotional response students have to learning that vocabulary may determine the long-term effect on vocabulary development, writing, and reading comprehension.

Summary of Research on the Meaning Vocabulary Component

There is renewed interest in the role of meaning vocabulary as we become aware of the discrepancies between the meaning vocabularies of advantaged children and children living in poverty or learning English. Teachers can greatly affect the size of their students' meaning vocabularies indirectly by promoting conversations, reading aloud to children, encouraging independent reading, and promoting word consciousness. Direct teaching of a limited number of important words and of word learning strategies can also result in larger vocabularies.

The major implication of this research on vocabulary may be to have a division of labor in teaching word meanings. While some direct teaching of general meaning vocabulary has a place, reading and writing instructional time may be better spent in teaching word learning strategies, promoting conversations about books, teacher read-aloud, and independent silent reading. On the other hand, content subjects such as science and social studies may be better venues for direct teaching of word meanings because of the natural opportunities for repeated and varied encounters with the words due to the organization of content instruction into extended units. Repeated exposure to words appears to be important for meaning vocabulary learning (Blachowicz and Fisher, 2000), and some research supports the importance of teaching prior knowledge along with word meanings (Baumann, Kame'enui, and Ash, 2003). If content subjects are the best place for most direct vocabulary teaching, an otherwise comprehensive literacy instructional program may be even more comprehensive if it leaves enough time for good science and social studies instruction than if it does not.

Writing Instruction

A comprehensive reading and writing program has two reasons to include effective writing instruction as a component. First, it cannot be a comprehensive reading and writing program without adequate quantity and quality of writing instruction. Second, there is evidence that good writing instruction also teaches children how to read better.

Teaching Children How to Write Better

The research on teaching writing is clear: grammar instruction does not result in students writing more correctly (Hillocks and Smith, 2003), and traditional, presentational instruction, where there are examinations of written models, specific writing assignments, and teacher feedback on that writing, has only small effects (Hillocks, 1986). Instead, natural process writing instruction is more effective, and what has been called environmental writing instruction, where students engage in various writing activities designed to teach them to learn and apply specific writing strategies and skills, is more effective still (Hillocks, 1986).

The key to teaching writing, including the conventions of writing, appears to include being consistent with a developmental sequence that recognizes the commonalities of children as they move from early emergence to sophisticated ability (Dyson and Freedman, 2003; Farnan and Dahl, 2003; Hodges, 2003). Effective writing programs will look very different, grade-by-grade, and will have expectations for children at each grade that are appropriate to their development as writers rather than arbitrary standards based on tradition or how officials would like to test writing. The best writing instruction will teach students how to plan, compose, revise, and edit their own pieces of writing, all within the context of inquiry, self-assessment, and self-regulation fostered by interaction with teachers and peers.

The Effect on Children's Reading of Learning How to Write Better

Earlier in this review, evidence was presented that spelling-based approaches to teaching phonics and word recognition in reading are effective. These approaches work best when the children write regularly so that they have many opportunities to apply what they are learning in spelling about both phonics and high-frequency words.

In her frequently cited review, Stotsky (1983) summarized a number of studies showing that better writers tend to be better readers. In the First-Grade Studies, classic research in reading education, Bond and Dykstra (1967/1997) concluded that reading programs with a writing component usually resulted in higher reading achievement by the end of first-grade than programs without a writing component. Mason, McDaniel, and Callaway (1974) found that first graders gained more in vocabulary knowledge and reading comprehension ability if they wrote regularly and tried to include the words they were being taught to read. Shanahan and Lomax (1986) found that first and second graders' work indicated an interactive relationship between reading and writing, that is, knowledge gained in one often transferred to the other.

A Word of Caution about Writing

While writing instruction can take too much time, that rarely occurs in our experience. Rather, the danger is that writing instruction will lose its value for either writing or reading improvement by focusing too much on preparing students for a high-stakes writing test. High-stakes writing tests definitely affect how writing is taught, and the effects often include a narrowing of the writing curriculum (Hillocks, 2002). Writing instruction can only fulfill its potential to help both writing and reading abilities develop if all major aspects and types of writing are taught in the elementary school writing curriculum.

Summary of the Research on the Writing Component

Good writing instruction teaches writing and, to a lesser extent, reading. Research on the development of writers can and should guide the instruction that children receive in the skills and strategies of writing and its parts.

A Final Word

American education has always been a very fadish institution, and reading and writing instruction has been the most fad-driven part of the curriculum. There is a huge body of research, conducted across decades, that supports the need for the components summarized in this review. Teachers and administrators should embrace this evidence and stand up for every child's right to a comprehensive reading and writing curriculum, from the beginning and throughout all the grades, that includes: word identification and comprehension instruction; daily time devoted to teacher read-aloud and independent reading; vocabulary instruction as part of reading instruction as well as science and social studies instruction; and instruction and time for writing both for its own sake and as another avenue through which children can become better readers.

References

Allington, R. L. (1977) If they don't read much, how are they ever gonna get good? *Journal of Reading, 21,* 57-61.

Allington, R. L. (1983) The reading instruction provided readers of differing reading abilities. *The Elementary School Journal, 83,* 548-559.

Allington, R. L. (1984) Content coverage and contextual reading in reading groups. *Journal of Reading Behavior, 16,* 85-96.

Anderson, R. C., Hiebert, E., Scott, J. and Wilkinson, I. (1985) *Becoming a Nation of Readers.* Washington, DC: National Institute of Education.

Armbruster, B. B., Lehr, F., and Osborn, J. (2001) *Put Reading First: The Research Building Blocks for Teaching Children to Read—Kindergarten through Grade 3.* Washington, DC: The Partnership for Reading.

Artley, S. L. (1975) Good teachers of reading: Who are they? *The Reading Teacher, 29,* 26-31.

Baumann, J. F., Kame'enui, E. J., and Ash, G. E. (2003) Research on vocabulary instruction: Voltaire redux. In J. Flood, D. Lapp, J. R. Squire, and J. M. Jensen (Eds.), *Handbook of Research on Teaching the English Language Arts, 2nd ed.* (pp. 752-785). Mahwah, NJ: Erlbaum.

Beck, I. L., McKeown, M. G. and Gromoll, E. W. (1989) Learning from social studies texts. *Cognition and Instruction, 6,* 99-158.

Beck, I. L., McKeown, M. G., Sandora, C., and Worthy, J. (1996) Questioning the author: A yearlong classroom implementation to engage students with text. *The Elementary School Journal, 96,* 385-414.

Becker, W. C. (1977) Teaching reading and language to the disadvantaged—What we have learned from field research. *Harvard Educational Review, 47,* 518-543.

Biemiller, A. (1977) Relationships between oral reading rates for letters, words, and simple text in the development of reading achievement. *Reading Research Quarterly, 13,* 223-253.

Biemiller, A., and Slonim, M. (2001) Estimating root word vocabulary growth in normative and advantaged populations: Evidence for a common sequence of vocabulary acquisition. *Journal of Educational Psychology, 93,* 498-520.

Blachowicz, C. L. Z., and Fisher, P. (2000) Vocabulary instruction. In M. L. Kamil, P. B. Mosenthal, P. D. Pearson, and R. Barr (Eds.), *Handbook of Reading Research* (Vol. III, pp. 503-523). Mahwah, NJ: Erlbaum.

Bond, G. L., and Dykstra, R. (1997) The cooperative research program in first-grade reading instruction. *Reading Research Quarterly, 32,* 345-428. (Original work published 1967)

Bosman, A. M. T., and Van Orden, G. C. (1997) Why spelling is more difficult than reading. In C. A. Perfetti, L. Rieben, and M. Fayol (Eds.), *Learning to Spell: Research, Theory, and Practice across Languages* (pp. 173-194). Mahwah, NJ: Erlbaum.

Bryant, P., and Bradley, L. (1980) Why children sometimes write words they cannot read. In U. Frith (Ed.), *Cognitive Processes in Spelling* (pp. 356-370). London: Academic Press.

Byrne, B., and Fielding-Barnsley, R. (1995) Evaluation of a program to teach phonemic awareness to young children: A 2- and 3-year follow-up and a new preschool trial. *Journal of Educational Psychology, 87,* 488-503.

Campbell, J., Voelkl, K. and Donahue, P. (1997) NAEP 1996 trends in academic progress. Washington, DC: National Center for Educational Statistics.

Carver, R. P. and Leibert, R. E. (1995) The effect of reading library books at different levels of difficulty upon gains in reading ability. *Reading Research Quarterly, 30,* 26-48.

Cataldo, S., and Ellis, N. (1988) Interactions in the development of spelling, reading and phonological skills. *Journal of Research in Reading, 11* (2), 86-109.

Catts, H. W., Fey, M. E., Zhang, X. and Tomblin, J. B. (1999) Language basis of reading and reading disabilities: Evidence from a longitudinal investigation. *Scientific Studies of Reading, 3*, 331-361.

Chasen, S. P. and Gambrell, L. B. (1992) A comparison of teacher read aloud practices and attitudes: 1980-1990. *Literacy: Issues and Practices, 9*, 29-32.

Cipielewski, J., and Stanovich, K. E. (1992) Predicting growth in reading ability from children's exposure to print. *Journal of Experimental Child Psychology, 54*, 74-89.

Clarke, L. K. (1988) Invented versus traditional spelling in first graders' writings: Effects on learning to spell and read. *Research in the Teaching of English, 22*, 281-309.

Cunningham, A. E. and Stanovich K. E. (1998) What reading does for the mind. *American Educator, 22* (1 and 2), 8-15.

Cunningham, A. E., Perry, K. E., and Stanovich, K. E. (2001) Converging evidence for the concept of orthographic processing. *Reading and Writing: An Interdisciplinary Journal, 14*, 549-568.

Cunningham, J. W. (1993) Whole-to-part reading diagnosis. *Reading and Writing Quarterly, 9*, 31-49.

Cunningham, J. W., Koppenhaver, D. A., Erickson, K. A., and Spadorcia, S. A. (in press) Word identification and text characteristics. In J. V. Hoffman and D. Schallert (Eds.), *Texts, Tasks and Teaching Reading in Elementary Classrooms.* Mahwah, NJ: Erlbaum.

Cunningham, P. M. (2000) *Phonics They Use, 3rd ed.* New York: Addison-Wesley.

Davis, L. H. (2000) The effects of rime-based analogy training on word reading and spelling of first-grade children with good and poor phonological awareness (Doctoral dissertation, Northwestern University, 2000) *Dissertation Abstracts International, 61*, 2253A.

Duke, N. K., and Pearson, P. D. (2002) Effective practices for developing reading comprehension. In A. E. Farstrup and S. J. Samuels (Eds.), *What Research Has to Say about Reading Instruction, 3rd ed.* (pp. 205-242) Newark, DE: International Reading Association.

Durkin, D. (1979) What classroom observations reveal about reading comprehension instruction. *Reading Research Quarterly, 14*, 481-533.

Dyson, A. H., and Freedman, S. W. (2003) Writing. In J. Flood, D. Lapp, J. R. Squire, and J. M. Jensen (Eds.), *Handbook of Research on Teaching the English Language Arts, 2nd ed.* (pp. 967-992) Mahwah, NJ: Erlbaum.

Ehri, L. C. (1997) Learning to read and learning to spell are one and the same, almost. In C. A. Perfetti, L. Rieben, and M. Fayol (Eds.), *Learning to Spell: Research, Theory, and Practice across Languages* (pp. 237-269). Mahwah, NJ: Erlbaum.

Ehri, L. C., and Wilce, L. (1987) Does learning to spell help beginners learn to read words? *Reading Research Quarterly, 22*, 47-65.

Elley, W. B. (1989) Vocabulary acquisition from listening to stories. *Reading Research Quarterly, 24*, 174-187.

Ellis, N., and Cataldo, S. (1990) The role of spelling in learning to read. *Language and Education, 4*, 47-76.

Erekson, J. A. (2001) Prosody and performance: Children talking the text in elementary school. (Doctoral dissertation, Michigan State University, 2001). *Dissertation Abstracts International, 62*, 947A.

Farnan, N., and Dahl, K. (2003) Children's writing: Research and practice. In J. Flood, D. Lapp, J. R. Squire, and J. M. Jensen (Eds.), *Handbook of Research on Teaching the English Language Arts, 2nd ed.* (pp. 993-1007). Mahwah, NJ: Erlbaum.

Gough, P. B., Juel, C., and Griffith, P. L. (1992) Reading, spelling, and the orthographic cipher. In P. B. Gough, L. Ehri, and R. Treiman (Eds.), *Reading Acquisition* (pp. 35-48). Hillsdale, NJ: Erlbaum.

Graves, M. F. and Watts-Taffe, S. M. (2002) The place of word consciousness in a research-based vocabulary program. In A. E. Farstrup and S. J. Samuels (Eds.), *What Research Has to Say about Reading Instruction, 3rd ed.* (pp. 140-165). Newark, DE: International Reading Association.

Gustafson, S. (2001) Cognitive abilities and print exposure in surface and phonological types of reading disability. *Scientific Studies of Reading, 5*, 351-375.

Hall, D. P. (1991) Investigating the relationship between word knowledge and cognitive ability (Doctoral dissertation, University of North Carolina at Greensboro, 1991). *Dissertation Abstracts International, 52*, 2873A.

Hart, B., and Risley, T. R. (1995) *Meaningful Differences in the Everyday Experiences of Young American Children.* Baltimore: Paul H. Brookes.

Hillocks, G., Jr. (1986) Research on written composition: New directions for teaching. Urbana, IL: National Conference on Research in English/ERIC Clearinghouse on Reading and Communication Skills.

Hillocks, G., Jr. (2002) *The Testing Trap: How State Writing Assessments Control Learning.* New York: Teachers College Press.

Hillocks, G., Jr., and Smith, M. W. (2003) Grammars and literacy learning. In J. Flood, D. Lapp, J. R. Squire, and J. M. Jensen (Eds.), *Handbook of Research on Teaching the English Language Arts, 2nd ed.* (pp. 721-737). Mahwah, NJ: Erlbaum.

Hodges, R. E. (2003) The conventions of writing. In J. Flood, D. Lapp, J. R. Squire, and J. M. Jensen (Eds.), *Handbook of Research on Teaching the English Language Arts, 2nd ed.* (pp. 1052-1063). Mahwah, NJ: Erlbaum.

Ivey G. and Broaddus, K. (2001) Just plain reading: A survey of what students want to read in middle school classrooms. *Reading Research Quarterly, 36*, 350-377.

Juel, C., Biancarosa, G., Coker, D., and Deffes, R. (2002, May) The importance of preschool and kindergarten language development in reading acquisition. Paper presented at the meeting of the International Reading Association, San Francisco, CA.

Juel, C., and Minden-Cupp, C. (2000) Learning to read words: Linguistic units and instructional strategies. *Reading Research Quarterly, 35*, 458-492.

Lee, C. H., Honig, R., and Lee, Y. (2002) Phonological recoding of mixed-case words in the priming task. *Reading Psychology, 23*, 199-216.

Lehman, B. A., Freeman, V. E and Allen, V. G. (1994) Children's literature and literacy instruction: Literature-based elementary teachers' beliefs and practices. *Reading Horizons, 35*, 3-29.

Logan, G. D. (1997) Automaticity and reading: Perspectives from the instance theory of automation. *Reading and Writing Quarterly, 13*, 123-146.

Mason, G., McDaniel, H., and Callaway, B. (1974) Relating reading and spelling: A comparison of methods. *Elementary School Journal, 74*, 381-386.

Morrow, L. M and Gambrell, L. B. (2000) Literature-based reading instruction. In M. L. Kamil, P. B. Mosenthal, P. D. Pearson, and R. Barr (Eds.), *Handbook of Reading Research* (Vol. III, pp. 563-586). Mahwah, NJ: Erlbaum.

Nagy, W. E. and Anderson. R. C. (1984) How many words are there in printed school English? *Reading Research Quarterly, 19*, 304-330.

Nagy, W. E., and Herman, P. A. (1987) Breadth and depth of vocabulary knowledge: Implications for acquisition and instruction. In M. G. McKeown and M. E. Curtis (Eds.), *The Nature of Vocabulary Acquisition* (pp.19-35). Hillsdale, NJ: Erlbaum.

National Reading Panel (2000a) Teaching children to read: An evidence-based assessment of the scientific research literature on reading and its implications for reading instruction (National Institute of Health Pub. No. 00-4769). Washington, DC: National Institute of Child Health and Human Development.

National Reading Panel (2000b) Teaching children to read: An evidence-based assessment of the scientific research literature on reading and its implications for reading instruction: Reports of the subgroups (National Institute of Health Pub. No. 00-4754). Washington, DC: National Institute of Child Health and Human Development.

Palinscar, A. S. and Brown, A. L. (1984) Interactive teaching to promote independent learning from text. *The Reading Teacher, 39*, 771-777.

Pearson, P. D., and Fielding, L. (1991) Comprehension instruction. In R. Barr, M. L. Kamil, P. B. Mosenthal, and P. D. Pearson (Eds.), *Handbook of Reading Research* (Vol. II, pp. 815-860). White Plains, NY: Longman.

Perfetti, C. A. (1997) The psycholinguistics of spelling and reading. In C. A. Perfetti, L. Rieben, and M. Fayol (Eds.), *Learning to Spell: Research, Theory, and Practice across Languages* (pp. 21-38). Mahwah, NJ: Erlbaum.

Pressley, M., Almasi, J., Schuder, T., Bergman, J., Hite, S., El-Dinary, P. B., et al. (1994) Transactional instruction of comprehension strategies: The Montgomery County, Maryland SAIL Program. *Reading and Writing Quarterly, 10*, 5-19.

Pressley, M. and Wharton-McDonald, R. (1998) The development of literacy, Part 4: The need for increased comprehension in upper-elementary grades. In M. Pressley (Ed.), *Reading Instruction that Works: The Case for Balanced Teaching* (pp. 192-227). New York: Guilford.

Samuels, S. J. (2002) Reading fluency: Its development and assessment. In A. E. Farstrup and S. J. Samuels (Eds.), *What Research Has to Say about Reading Instruction, 3rd ed.* (pp. 166-183). Newark, DE: International Reading Association.

Shanahan, T., and Lomax, R. (1986) An analysis and comparison of theoretical models of the reading-writing relationship. *Journal of Educational Psychology, 78*, 116-123.

Shankweiler, D. (1999) Words to meanings. *Scientific Studies of Reading, 3*, 113-127.

Share, D. L. (1995) Phonological recoding and self-teaching: Sine qua non of reading acquisition. *Cognition, 55*, 151-218.

Share, D. L. (1999) Phonological recoding and orthographic learning: A direct test of the self-teaching hypothesis. *Journal of Experimental Child Psychology, 72*, 95-129.

Stahl, S. A., Duffy-Hester, A. M., Stahl, K. A. D. (1998) Everything you wanted to know about phonics (but were afraid to ask). *Reading Research Quarterly, 33*, 338-355.

Stahl, S. A., Richek, M. A., and Vandevier, R. J. (1991) Learning meaning vocabulary through listening: A sixth-grade replication. *Learner Factors/Teacher Factors: Issues in Literacy Research and Instruction* (40th Yearbook of the National Reading Conference; pp. 185-192). Chicago: National Reading Conference.

Stanovich, K. E. (1986) Matthew effects in reading: Some consequences of individual differences in the acquisition of literacy. *Reading Research Quarterly, 21*, 360-401.

Stanovich, K. E., and West, R. F. (1989) Exposure to print and orthographic processing. *Reading Research Quarterly, 24*, 402-433.

Stotsky, S. (1983) Research on reading/writing relationships: A synthesis and suggested directions. *Language Arts, 60*, 627-642.

Tierney, R. J., and Cunningham, J. W. (1984) Research on teaching reading comprehension. In P. D. Pearson, R. Barr, M. L. Kamil, and P. Mosenthal (Eds.), *Handbook of Reading Research* (Vol. 1, pp. 609-655). White Plains, NY: Longman.

Topping, K., and Paul, T. (1999) Computer-assisted assessment of practice at reading: A large scale survey using Accelerated Reader data. *Reading and Writing Quarterly, 15*, 213-231.

Torgesen, J. K., and Davis, C. (1996) Individual difference variables that predict response to training in phonological awareness. *Journal of Experimental Child Psychology, 63*, 1-21.

Torgesen, J. K., Wagner, R. K., and Rashotte, C. A. (1997) Prevention and remediation of severe reading disabilities: Keeping the end in mind. *Scientific Studies of Reading, 1*(3), 217-234.

Uhry, J. K., and Shepherd, M. J. (1993) Segmentation/spelling instruction as part of a first-grade reading program: Effects on several measures of reading. Reading Research Quarterly, 28, 218-233.

Wise, B. W., and Olson, R. K. (1995) Computer-based phonological awareness and reading instruction. *Annals of Dyslexia, 45*, 99-122.

Yopp, H. K., and Yopp, R. H. (2000) Supporting phonemic awareness development in the classroom. *The Reading Teacher, 54*, 130-143.

Zutell, J. (1992) An integrated view of word knowledge: Correlational studies of the relationships among spelling, reading, and conceptual development. In S. Templeton and D. R. Bear (Eds.), *Development of Orthographic Knowledge and the Foundations of Literacy* (pp. 213-230). Hillsdale, NJ: Erlbaum.

Notes

The Administrator's Guide to the Four Blocks® © Carson-Dellosa CD-2425